A Kit Bag for Promoting Positive Behaviour in the Classroom

by the same author

Quick, Easy and Effective Behaviour Management Ideas for the Classroom
Nicola S. Morgan
ISBN 978 1 84310 951 8

of related interest

Count Me In!
Ideas for Actively Engaging Students in Inclusive Classrooms
Richard Rose and Michael Shevlin
Foreword by Paul Cooper
ISBN 978 1 84310 955 6
Part of the *Innovative Learning for All* series

How to Help Children and Young People with Complex Behavioural Difficulties
A Guide for Practitioners Working in Educational Settings
Ted Cole and Barbara Knowles
Foreword by Joan Pritchard
ISBN 978 1 84905 049 4

Promoting Emotional Education
Engaging Children and Young People with Social, Emotional and Behavioural Difficulties
Edited by Carmel Cefai and Paul Cooper
ISBN 978 1 84310 996 9
Part of the *Innovative Learning for All* series

Helping Children to Cope with Change, Stress and Anxiety
A Photocopiable Activities Book
Deborah M. Plummer
Illustrated by Alice Harper
ISBN 978 1 84310 960 0

Creative Coping Skills for Children
Emotional Support through Arts and Crafts Activities
Bonnie Thomas
ISBN 978 1 84310 921 1

A Kit Bag for Promoting Positive Behaviour in the Classroom

Nicola S. Morgan and Gillian Ellis

Jessica Kingsley *Publishers*
London and Philadelphia

First published in 2011
by Jessica Kingsley Publishers
116 Pentonville Road
London N1 9JB, UK
and
400 Market Street, Suite 400
Philadelphia, PA 19106, USA

www.jkp.com

Library of Congress Cataloging in Publication Data
Morgan, Nicola S.
  A kit bag for promoting positive behaviour in the classroom / Nicola S Morgan and Gillian Ellis.
     p. cm.
  Includes bibliographical references and index.
  ISBN 978-1-84905-213-9 (alk. paper)
  1. Classroom management. 2. Problem children--Behavior modification. I. Ellis, Gillian. II. Title.
  LB3013.M6655 2011
  371.102'4--dc22
                                        2011003018

British Library Cataloguing in Publication Data
A CIP catalogue record for this book is available from the British Library

ISBN 978 1 84905 213 9

Printed and bound in Great Britain

To my dad, thank you for all your
support, enthusiasm and love
(Nicola S. Morgan)

To my family for showing the values of patience, tolerance
and love and to my dad for always believing in me
(Gillian Ellis)

Contents

Introduction

The best way to make children good is to make them happy

Oscar Wilde

The inspiration for writing this book came when, as qualified teachers ourselves, we were faced with children with challenging behaviour in school and found that there was a real lack of material that offered effective solutions to specific problems in the classroom.

We have found from experience that as teachers we can have the best curriculum planning, an abundance of wonderful teaching resources and excellent subject knowledge but this will be totally ineffective if behaviour management has not been given the same priority. Good behaviour management needs to be embedded into the daily routines of the classroom with clear expectations set from the outset. Behaviour management is the one area which cannot be glossed over and given a quick fix; we need to peel back the layers and fully understand the reasons why these behaviours are occurring in the first place before we can apply a solution. We also need to recognise that all children are different and one solution does not fit all.

You are probably wondering at this point who the authors of this book are, so here is a short introduction to the both of us. My name is Nicola S. Morgan and I have worked in a variety of schools providing teachers with hands-on practical tips and solutions for the most challenging children. My interest in behaviour management began when I was a teacher in the classroom. I was in a school with a high percentage of children who displayed challenging behaviour and I realised that by using a positive approach I could change behaviour. This transformation had the most amazing results not only on the individual children but also on my classroom. By using positive strategies and techniques I created a place where I enjoyed teaching and my class loved to learn! It was with this passion that I decided to become an independent consultant so that I could share hands-on practical, behaviour management strategies with other schools and authorities.

I am Gillian Ellis, currently headteacher of a large primary school in South Wales. Nicola was recommended to me after I was faced with some challenging behaviours in my school. Together, we worked with staff and involved children and parents/carers in creating a school which I am happy to say is now calm, positive and reflective. Nicola's practical approach to behaviour management was like a breath of fresh air!

We both have a passion for creating the right environment for every child to develop and grow. Therefore, this book was written with the sole purpose of giving teachers a set of tools which could be applied simply and easily to any classroom. It has been written to support teachers in creating a classroom where children want to learn and teachers are excited about teaching. We have tried to give a solution to every single type of behaviour that teachers face on a daily basis in the classroom. So, whether you are a newly qualified teacher straight from university or an experienced teacher with a wealth of expertise we hope that you find this book useful.

So, now we have established why this book was written we now need to explain the best way to use this book. After a lot of thought we decided that we wanted a book which could be used as a directory so that when a teacher is faced with a particular behaviour a solution can be found very quickly at the touch of her fingertips! With this thought in mind the book has been split into seven chapters with each chapter covering ideas to manage a set of related behaviours, which we have called tools. Each tool has been tried and tested in classrooms with the most challenging of children. At the beginning of each tool the behaviour is identified and then a bank of practical strategies is given to provide solutions to that particular behaviour. There is also a simple five-step self-assessment checklist which we advise that you use before you begin to implement an individual tool. This will provide you with all the information you need to achieve ultimate success. All the tools are about behaviours with which teachers are challenged on a daily basis. This ranges from low-level to high-level challenging behaviour.

At the end of each tool are suggestions for next steps. These are to support you to ensure that the tools are sustainable and produce the results you want. There is also a useful resource list at the back of the book, which will help you either research more information about a particular behaviour or give a reference to practical resources to support the tools.

The idea of a 'kit bag', in which the ideas for managing the different behaviours, which we call tools, can be picked and mixed, we believe to be innovative. We hope that it will provide you with no-nonsense, hands-on practical solutions which will help in the classroom. The kit bag can be used for finding a solution to a one-off problem or for dipping in and out of as and when needed. It could also be used if you are looking to take a fresh approach to your classroom teaching or if you are a supply teacher working in different schools.

The chapters have been collated under the following five headings:

- Creating a positive learning environment
- Positive classroom management
- Re-focusing
- Confidence building
- Challenging behaviour

The first two chapters explain how to create a positive environment. We cannot emphasise enough that the setting within the classroom is crucial to the effectiveness of the tools. There are lots of handy tips and ideas of how to do this. We aim to give a real insight into how you can transform your classroom into one that is inspirational.

We know that throughout the academic year classrooms develop and change and there are reasons for these changes. A positive classroom environment can very quickly change into a classroom that is challenging and out of control. As teachers we need to be proactive to these changes and keep one step ahead. Below we have given three ways of how the book can be used in supporting change within the classroom.

Scenario 1

It's the start of a new academic year, you have a new class and you are conscious that some of the children in the class are challenging in terms of their behaviour. How do you set the right expectations for teaching and learning to take place for the forthcoming year?

For a solution to the scenario we have picked a selection of tools which you can mix and use.

Tool 6 Establishing effective routines

- Symbols
- Routine to the beat

Tool 5 Positive reinforcements

- Secret student
- Raffle tickets

Tool 3 Effective rules

- Move to the right!
- The jigsaw rules display

Tool 4 Effective correctives

- Time-out
- The planets

Tool 14 Getting the children's attention

- Silence all around
- Can you hear the music?

Tool 24 Helping the child who is not following direction

- Scripts
- Visual signs

Scenario 2

You are a supply teacher and you have been asked to teach a class which you know is challenging and on your last supply day one of the children walked out of the classroom and was rude to you. You have been asked to supply at the school again but you are concerned that you will not be able to control the class. What do you do?

Selection of tools to use and try:

Tool 7 Helping children to enter the classroom successfully

- Not ready to come into my classroom?

Tool 13 Helping children to leave the classroom successfully

- Staggered dismissal

Tool 14 Getting the children's attention

- The rhythm game

Tool 18 Preventing children from calling out

- Asking questions

Tool 24 Helping the child who is not following direction

- Choices

Scenario 3

You have worked hard since the beginning of the year to establish clear rules and expectations for all your pupils. Your headteacher has asked you to take on a new addition to your class. After a couple of days the new child is displaying attention-seeking behaviour. What do you do?

Selection of tools to use and try:

Tool 17 Addressing attention-seeking behaviour

- Top Time

- Certificates

Tool 18 Preventing children from calling out

- Ignoring the behaviour

Tool 20 Supporting the child who lacks self-esteem

- Look what I can do!

Tool 21 Supporting the child who lacks friends

- Friendship groups

Please note that to avoid any gender bias the gender pronoun is used interchangeably throughout the book. We hope that you enjoy using our book in your classroom and find it to be an invaluable tool. We would both love to hear how you get on and you can email us at: info@behaviourstop.co.uk

PART I

CREATING A POSITIVE LEARNING ENVIRONMENT

The behaviour

Whilst this is a book to provide you with effective tools for behaviour management in the classroom, it cannot go unnoted that the most effective classrooms are influenced by the positive learning environment of the setting it is within, i.e. the school. As soon as you walk into a school you cannot only see the ethos from its displays and colours but you can feel it. The entrance to a school is an important statement for any visitor. It shows very quickly what your vision is as a school and the message that it is trying to convey. It is without question that what goes on outside your classroom has an impact on you and the pupils you teach.

Does your school promote a positive learning environment?

SELF-ASSESSMENT CHECKLIST

As teachers we are constantly faced with challenges every day and providing solutions to these challenges is not an easy task. Sometimes, however hard we try, certain situations push our professionalism to the limit. When this happens we need to take a deep breath and ask ourselves some basic questions as to why these things are happening.

Here is a simple five-step checklist to do a quick self-assessment for any situation which you may face in the classroom. If you can answer all these questions then you know that you have got the basics covered and can go ahead with finding the right tool to fit the right behaviour. Spending a short time doing this before you implement the tool will ensure that you achieve ultimate success.

Step 1 Check the history

Play detective and find out all you can about the behaviour and the child. It may mean finding out what her behaviour was like the previous year, meeting with her class teacher or phoning up her previous school. Gather as much information as you can. What strategies were previously used? Was there parental involvement? Attendance record? Friendship groups? Academic performance?

Step 2 Check by establishing the 'Why?'

There is always a reason behind every behaviour. Behaviour is a form of communication; sometimes children (and adults) find it difficult to communicate how they are feeling because they don't know what words to use and find it easier to act out the way they feel which can sometimes result in unwanted behaviour. This behaviour is an indication that something is not right and/or their needs are not being met.

By observing and talking to the child and, if appropriate, to her parent(s)/carer(s), you can start to piece together the 'behaviour jigsaw puzzle' in order to create the big picture and establish why she is behaving in this way. When the 'why?'

has been established you can then help her to understand and manage that behaviour.

Step 3 Check positive reinforcement

Make sure that the child knows you care about her. Remember that she may have taken a long time to develop this behaviour, so be consistent and patient as the behaviour takes time to change. Establishing a good relationship with a child shows that you are interested in her and promotes her self-esteem. Remember that behaviours occur for a reason and children who display challenging behaviour do not have the skills that adults have in dealing with situations. Are you using positive language? Are your positive reinforcements exciting and motivational? Do your rewards excite and motivate children? Are you consistent in your approach?

Step 4 Check class rules

Rules create clear expectations for children and define what is acceptable behaviour. Are your class rules clear and do all the children in the class understand and respect them? Are they brightly and prominently displayed, and reinforced on a regular basis?

Step 5 Check correctives

Are you consistent in your approach to implementing your correctives within the classroom? Do children see this as fair? Children usually respect fair play. Are your correctives fair, consistent and a logical and realistic response to the behaviour?

Tool 1

A Whole-School Approach

All good schools aim to create an inclusive culture which is positive and which meets both the demands of the curriculum and the emotional wellbeing of all its staff and pupils. Sometimes, despite these efforts, challenging behaviour displayed in the classroom does impede on the learning of others. Challenging behaviour is usually displayed for a reason and whilst schools work relentlessly to support all their pupils as individuals, unwanted and challenging behaviour is never and cannot be acceptable.

All pupils have a right to the opportunity to learn without the interference or disruption of others to enable them to grow into confident, independent lifelong learners. However, the reality of creating a school where equal opportunities occurs for every single pupil is a difficult one, particularly when challenging behaviour becomes the focus of attention for staff on a daily basis and distracts them from delivering the high-quality learning they are seeking.

It is well documented that schools struggle to achieve a constant juggling act between trying to create a sense of equilibrium for all their staff and pupils in establishing a culture in which everyone benefits and is successful whilst at the same time meeting individual pupils' needs, especially those children with additional learning needs. Changing the culture of a school is a long and strategic process. To change the culture of a school all staff and pupils must have a strong vision for school effectiveness. To this end, the importance of implementing effective behaviour management systems is crucial if schools are to turn their vision successfully into a reality.

A whole-school behaviour policy

All good schools have an effective behaviour policy which provides clear guidelines for all its stakeholders and sets out its rules, correctives and rewards and how to implement and monitor them.

There are many examples of good behaviour policies available within local authorities in the UK and on the internet if you require one. A good policy is supported by a good behaviour management system. One with which we have worked successfully in schools is 'The five-step behaviour programme' which is comprehensive and includes a whole-school step-by-step approach.

Creating a positive learning culture

The culture of a school has a huge impact on how people in them learn, behave, respect one another and develop as independent learners. This is achieved by developing and implementing:

- effective sanctions
- positive reinforcements
- shared beliefs
- traditions, practices and rituals
- positive, supportive school community.

School's vision

Successful schools have a clear sense of direction and vision. When creating a vision for your school it is important to decide the type of school you seek to become. Involve all members of the school community in creating a shared vision for your school, taking into consideration the agreed set of core beliefs to which the school community can commit.

Creating a shared vision:

- identify and share the school's core beliefs
- describe how your ideal school would look
- implement.

Ethos and values

How people feel and think about the place in which they learn and teach makes a difference to how they do their job. Therefore, the school's ethos and values need to be deep-rooted and promoted for all to see.

Tool 2

A Positive Approach

For an environment to stay positive teachers need to keep themselves motivated. A whole-school culture where staff are nurtured and relationships are fostered is a culture which is warm, friendly and respectful. This is an environment in which teachers feel valued and therefore value others. Being recognised for what you do is a great motivator! There are some great motivating tips around and some of the best can be found on a website called MotivatingMates.com. This website will give you a daily motivating quote that will inspire you and others.

The golden rules of teaching

Teaching children and managing sometimes difficult situations is never an easy job. Teaching can sometimes become stressful even for the most accomplished teacher. It is vitally important that you think and feel as if you are in control all the time. Positive attitudes are contagious. By being positive, you will affect and change the children's outlook within the class in an empathetic and forward-looking manner. Never let the children know that you have doubts in your own ability or are unable to cope in particular situations. Exude confidence at all times.

1. Believe that you have the ability to manage a class effectively.

2. Celebrate all your achievements, however small.

3. Understand that you are human and that you will make mistakes. Remember, mistakes are merely the portals to learning.

4. Keep a flexible approach and do what works best for you and the children.

5. Adopt a sense of humour and have some fun!

You as the teacher

The heart of effective behaviour management is building positive relationships with children. This allows you to connect to the child forming a strong foundation from which behavioural change can take place.

There are a number of ways to build a strong and respectful relationship with the class. These include:

1. being a positive role model for the children; for them to be respectful to others they must be treated with respect

2. creating a caring, supportive and fair environment where each child feels accepted and where he feels that he belongs and is relaxed

3. recognising every child's strengths and believing that every child has the ability to learn (especially pupils with special educational needs and disabilities)

4. acknowledging, reinforcing and sharing all successes with the class

5. taking time to speak to each child individually to find out about his interests, talents, goals, likes and dislikes

6. discussing classroom rules and sanctions so that all children are clear and understand what is expected of them

7. when using reprimands never embarrassing or ridiculing the children

8. interacting with the children during playtime (e.g., joining in a game of football or 'hopscotch') or by just having a chat. Children naturally enjoy this kind of interaction and it helps to give them confidence. You are also showing them that you have a genuine 'care' for their needs.

Get to know them

If you are a new teacher or are given a new class, it is important to get to know the children as soon as possible. One way of achieving this is to give your children a clean sheet of paper. Then ask them to write answers to the following questions.

1. What is your name?

2. What is your birthday?

3. Who are your best friend/s in the class?

4. What are your favourite television programmes?

5. What is your favourite kind of music?

6. Who are your favourite singers or groups?

7. What are your outside school interests (e.g. what you like doing at weekends or in school holidays)?

8. What are the names of your pets and what type of animal, fish or insect (e.g. dog, cat, hamster) are they?

9. What are the first names of your parent(s) or carer(s)?

10. Where do you like to go on holiday or where would you like to go?

11. What is your favourite football or rugby team or your favourite sport or pastime?

12. What are your favourite foods?

13. What are your biggest dislikes?

14. What is your favourite activity/subject in school?

15. What is your idea for a school/classroom trip?

Tool 3

Effective Rules

Rules create clear boundaries and expectations for all pupils and define what is acceptable behaviour. These must be reinforced on a regular basis and have a dedicated display within the classroom which is visible for all the class to see. It is essential that children should be involved in creating the class rules as this will give them ownership and they will be more likely to accept their terms and conditions and therefore comply.

THE TOOLS

Establishing rules

The first lesson of a new school year should be on establishing expectations and creating classroom rules. This lesson will be a good step towards creating a positive learning environment in which children can flourish and learn. There should be no more than five class rules; and there should be fewer for a class in foundation phase. Keep the words simple and in words that all children can understand.

When designing classroom rules make sure that they are clear, comprehensive and enforceable. Write the rules in a positive way and avoid using 'don'ts'. For example, 'I will walk sensibly around the school', rather than 'Don't run around the school'. Pupils require understandable directions. Hence, the rules need to be specific and explainable, for example, telling pupils to 'Be good' or 'Don't do that' is too vague. Here is an example of a set of classroom rules taken from one of the schools with which we have worked:

- Keep hands, feet, objects and unkind words to yourself.

- Follow instructions straight away.

- Be ready when an adult signals for attention.

- Use the correct voice level.
- Respect one another, equipment and the environment.

An adaptation of the above rules for foundation phase are as follows:

- Treat everyone and everything kindly.
- Listen when an adult is talking to you.
- Follow instructions straight away.
- Respect everyone and everything.

Pupil voice

It is important to include the children in formulating the rules as this gives them ownership and they'll be more likely to reinforce them.

Board game rules

Arrange the children in small groups to design a board game based on a class theme. They are then asked to present the game to the class and in doing so discuss the rules of the game and why rules are important. When they have completed this task the class are then asked in their groups to think of rules for the class.

Move to the right!

In small groups, ask the children to write down six rules and, once they have completed this, ask them to pass their paper to the person on their right. This child puts a star next to the rule she feels is the most important. The paper continues to pass to the right again until the child receives her original sheet. The children are then asked to read out their starred rules and these are written on the classroom board. The children are then asked to agree with the rules and to prioritise them. If anyone feels strongly about a rule she has to give a reason why she thinks the class should keep it.

Positive pupil

In groups, ask the children to make a list of the characteristics of a pupil who behaves in a positive way. Each group feeds back and a master list is created and displayed in the classroom.

Symbols

I make rules & symbols

When the class rules have been established ask the children to design a symbol for each rule. These symbols can be displayed around the classroom to remind the children to make the right choices. Symbols are an effective way for communication, especially for children with learning disabilities, or for those on the autistic spectrum.

Reinforcing the rules

It is important to reinforce the classroom rules on a daily basis, especially during the start of a new term. This also helps to check the children's understanding of the rules and gives the opportunity to explain the rationale behind them. The following are some tips for reinforcing your classroom rules.

Questions underneath

Write the rules of the class that you want to reinforce on pieces of card and bluetack them under the children's tables. The rules are written in question format, for example, 'When can I leave the classroom to go to the toilet?' When it's time to reinforce the rules, ask the children to look under their tables and in turn read out a question. This question is then answered either by the teacher or a pupil.

Solve the rules equation

On the board write an equation based on the first letter of each class rule for the children to complete, for example:

Follow instructions first time

Keep hands, feet, objects and unkind words to ourselves

Respect one another and our surroundings

Be ready when an adult signals for attention

Use correct voice level

F + K + R + B + U = Our class rules

Classroom positive behaviour hotspot

The classroom positive behaviour hotspot is a great way to focus children to help them to understand and remember a class rule. Each week identify a behaviour hotspot from one of your class rules and display it in the classroom on a large strip of paper for all the class to see. For example, when reinforcing the rule 'Use the correct voice level', if a child within the class is seen to demonstrate this rule she is positively reinforced with praise or a reward. This can also be adapted to other behaviours in the classroom.

The jigsaw rules display

When the class rules have been established, a great way to display them is by using a jigsaw theme. If your class has five rules draw a jigsaw puzzle with six pieces. On each piece write down the class rules and on the centre jigsaw piece write, for example, 'Can you complete the jigsaw?'

Photo shoot!

Everyone in the class has to play detective and spot anyone reinforcing a class rule. Photographs are then taken and displayed within the classroom to show others. This way the children in your class are becoming the role models for other children.

Tips for supply teachers

Unless you have a regular supply teacher who is familiar with your class routines, remembering all the class rules can be confusing. To help supply teachers or teaching assistants stick to one rule and one rule only, use the 'Listen and Do!' rule for effective behaviour management.

'Listen and Do!'

Keep it simple, keep to one rule: 'Listen and Do!' The one thing that teachers need children to do in the classroom is to listen to them. Children need to listen to instructions by the teacher so that they can engage in learning and abide by school routines such as breaks and assembly times.

This rule must be reinforced at regular times throughout the day in the form of a game, the 'Listen and Do!' game. To implement this strategy you need to turn it into a game. Start by giving each table a card numbered from 1 to 7 (depending on the number of tables or groups in the class) which corresponds to the number on a large sheet of paper. The teacher says, 'Listen and Do! Put your books away.' The table to put away their books first wins a point on the 'Listen and Do!' chart, which is displayed in a prominent place in the classroom.

Each column has four coloured sections, each representing different sessions of the day, for example blue=first lesson, yellow=fourth lesson. The table who reaches the star first wins the game. It is advisable that the teacher paces the game so that just before the end of the day one table or group reaches the star. It is up to the teacher in charge what rewards are given to the winning table. Celebrate and motivate tables' progress throughout the day, for example 'Well done, table 3, you are in the lead; I wonder which table is going to be in the lead after this lesson? Remember, all you have to do is follow my direction when you hear the words "Listen and Do!"' A rewards chart could be used so that each group or table can choose a reward at the end of the day.

Tool 4

Effective Correctives

Correctives are only effective when used in the context of a positive classroom culture, where there are clear rules and routines as well as the use of rewards to reinforce the positive behaviour. The one message in achieving good behaviour management is to use a consistent approach. It must be made clear to the class that if a rule which they created is broken then there has to be a corrective implemented so that the child can be given every chance to reflect on his actions. Encouraging children to make the right choices and to keep the class rules is always a number one priority! A consistent approach sends a positive message to the children in your class. Correctives need to be timely, specific, logical, reasonable and fair, with a clear beginning and ending.

It is important that correctives are:

- understood by pupils, staff and parents/carers
- fair
- consistent
- a logical response to a behaviour
- realistic to the misbehaviour displayed.

Correctives should be implemented if a child breaks class rules and the consequence of breaking the rule involves the following:

- affecting the education and wellbeing of other pupils
- preventing the teacher from teaching
- comprising the safety of themselves or others
- a serious incident above and beyond the normal class rule.

The types of correctives issued need to be reasonable and proportional to the circumstances of the case; if they are too severe, delayed or inconsistent they will probably fail to work. The best way to reinforce class rules is if the children are involved in a discussion around what happens if a class rule is broken. Below are some ideas for a corrective list:

- a reminder
- a verbal warning
- time-out
- withdrawal of access to the school IT system (if the pupil misuses it by, for example, accessing an inappropriate website)
- prevent participation in non-curriculum activities; for example, Friday Fun
- five minutes off break time
- removal of break or lunchtime privileges
- parental involvement
- loss of privileges such as being a school council member or class monitor.

THE TOOLS

Give them a choice

Giving a child a choice helps him feel that he has a degree of control, which is all part of encouraging children to begin to take responsibility for their actions. When giving a child a choice decide on the choices which give the desired outcome; for example, if a child is playing with a toy car during a lesson you can say, 'Either put your toy car in your drawer, or put it on my desk.' Always give a choice and deliver the choice at their level so that you can have direct eye contact. When the choice has been given walk away from him giving him enough time and space to make that choice. A child is likely to display unwanted behaviour if you remain in close proximity to him and still give him eye contact.

Again, if there are clear rules in place every child will know that if he makes the wrong choice a consequence will be attached to it and there will be no surprises. The ownership for the action is put back on the child. This way, we are encouraging children to take responsibility for their actions and to manage their own behaviour.

When to reprimand

Early intervention, which is timely and specific before behavioural problems become too pronounced, is essential. When a child displays unwanted behaviour that requires a reprimand, do this quickly and then re-direct immediately, before the level of unwanted behaviour escalates.

Time-out

Time-out is an effective way to deal with unwanted behaviour, providing it is implemented before the behaviour becomes challenging. Time-out gives the child the opportunity to calm down and reflect on the unacceptable behaviour.

The children in your class should be made aware where the time-out area is in the classroom; the area should be easily accessible so that you can monitor the area when a child is in time-out. Putting a child outside of the classroom or somewhere where you cannot monitor the time-out is not acceptable. Ideally, the area could be a corner of the classroom, which is away from the door and the carpet area. Some schools use a round rubber coloured mat or even a hoop for a child to stand or sit in. Whatever is used all the children must understand and know where the area is and what it is to be used for. A good guide for the length of time a child is put into time-out could be according to his age; for example, a six-year-old would be put into time-out for six minutes. The use of an egg timer to regulate time spent is not recommended. We have found from our experience that children concentrate on watching the timer instead of focusing on reflecting on their behaviour. Also, it has been known for a child to announce to the teacher that he has finished his time-out! It is up to the teacher to decide when they think that a child is ready to join the class or group and not the child.

Time-out procedure to follow

When giving a child a choice it is important to deliver the choice at his level so that you can have direct eye contact. When the choice has been given, walk away from the child giving him enough time and space to make that choice. A child is likely to display unwanted behaviour if you remain in close proximity to the child and still give him eye contact.

- Ask the child to think about his behaviour.

- Remind the child of the rewards, activities, games, etc. taking place in the class.

- Inform the child that when you feel he is calm you will ask him if he is ready to re-join the class/group.

- Remember to praise the child when he re-joins the class/group sensibly.

- Implement the 'Five-minute golden rule'.

The 'Five-minute golden rule'

This rule works wonders for children who have displayed inappropriate behaviour. When you have needed to reprimand a child for an unwanted behaviour, the risk is that the child could then feel that he has 'blown it' and then lose the motivation to be good. So, in order to keep the child focused and motivated, implement the 'Five-minute golden rule'. Within five minutes of the reprimand, find something about which to praise the child; for example, sitting correctly, reading quietly, completing his work, putting his hand up to ask a question. This is very effective at keeping the child motivated to engage in appropriate behaviour.

The planets

To represent the planets cut out three large circles of card, one green, one orange and one red. Allocate each child a picture of a rocket with his name on and place all the rockets on the green planet. If a child displays unwanted behaviour ask him to move his rocket to the orange planet and encourage him to think about making positive choices, for example, if he is deliberately throwing sand on the floor.

If the child continues to display unwanted behaviour ask him to place his rocket on the red planet and put him into Time-out (see 'Time-out procedure to follow'). Whether the child is on the orange or red planet, as soon as he displays positive behaviour he is immediately moved back to the green planet. This is a good visual reminder; for young children you could display a picture of each of them as an astronaut on the card.

Class meeting

Class meetings can be utilised to discuss a number of different things. A useful thing to discuss in these meetings is responsibility-taking. Here, if there have been any behavioural incidents that week (it is helpful to hold the meetings weekly otherwise the children may forget past incidents) they can be discussed and reflected upon in the meeting in a non-threatening, non-blaming and reassuring way. Incidents of good behaviour are also discussed in these meetings, and rewards given. Class meetings need to be a regular occurrence so that the children don't think of them as only occurring in response to a behavioural incident. This would then make the meetings threatening.

The teacher decides what incidents will be discussed in the meeting, usually choosing one or two negative incidents and about two or three examples of good behaviour. All the children are encouraged to comment on the incidents discussed. The child (or children) who were involved in an incident are asked to listen as the class discuss it. The children reflect upon the following, led by the teacher:

1. What happened?
2. What could have led to the incident?
3. How did it make the class feel?
4. How could it be prevented from happening again?
5. What can we all learn from this?

Examples of good behaviour are discussed in the same way, but point 4 above is changed to 'How could this behaviour be encouraged to occur more often?'

Repairing the relationship

When a child has been given a class or playground warning card it is important to repair the relationship between adult and child as soon as possible. By repairing the relationship the child will be less likely to engage in unwanted behaviour. There are two ways to do this:

- If the child is returned to class after displaying unwanted behaviour here is a script you can use:

'Thank you for apologising and I can see that you're ready to make the right choice. I'm pleased you're going to re-join the class/group.'

- If the child has been given a corrective, implement the 'Five-minute golden rule'. Within five minutes of the reprimand, find something about which to praise the child; for example, sitting correctly, reading quietly, completing his work, putting his hand up to ask a question. This is very effective at keeping the child motivated to engage in appropriate behaviour.

Tool 5

Positive Reinforcements

Positive reinforcements encourage positive behaviour, therefore, every day needs to include a series of positive reinforcements to help focus the children and to create a calm positive environment in your classroom. When they follow instructions correctly we need to make sure that the behaviour happens again and again so that it becomes a habit. This forms the basis of human behaviour and motivation, and can be used effectively to encourage children to acquire skills and develop appropriate behaviour. To be effective rewards need to be something to which the pupils aspire to and want. Pupils in the foundation phase will desire different rewards from pupils in what is in the UK known as Key Stage 2.

When recognising and rewarding appropriate behaviour it is important to celebrate with high energy and to include the rest of the class, teaching assistant, other teachers and non-teaching staff. This energy is addictive and a child is likely to repeat the process again in order to get the same reaction. Do not put energy and time into inappropriate behaviour but instead deal with the situation in a calm manner, away from others, then re-direct her attention. As soon as the child displays appropriate behaviour celebrate with motivational and dynamic energy. The child will soon appreciate the different energies and act accordingly for a positive outcome.

1. Immediately reward behaviour you wish to see.

2. Consistently reward to help maintain the desired behaviour.

3. Ensure that the rewards are achievable to help maintain attention and motivation.

4. Make sure all children are fairly rewarded during the school day.

Frequency and level of rewards

The frequency and level of rewards given to children depends on the level of behaviour. If a child is displaying frequent and quite difficult to manage behaviour, then the frequency and level of reward must be high for the class. A class which has a high level of reward and motivates children is one which has low levels of inappropriate behaviour.

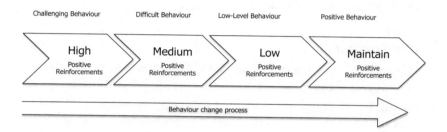

Effective praise

1. Make sure you define the appropriate behaviour when giving praise.

2. Praise should be given immediately following the desired behaviour.

3. Vary the ways in which you praise.

4. Relate praise to effort.

5. Encourage perseverance and independence.

6. *Do not* give praise continuously and without reason.

7. Be sincere when praising.

8. Never give praise and follow it with immediate criticism.

Role modelling

Model the desired behaviours that you would like to see in a child. Children are like sponges and learn a lot from watching others. So, if a teacher wants a child to tell the truth about a mistake she herself has made she should demonstrate this; for example, 'Sorry child A, I took your pen without asking you first; please accept my apology.' We underestimate the power of role modelling to children. Teachers need to take the first step in role modelling desired behaviours to children and then individual children themselves will start to role model to others within the class.

Good manners

Manners not only make a good impression on others but also make us feel good about ourselves. As well as opening doors for others and saying 'Good morning', modelling manners encourages children to treat others with similar respect. Always acknowledge and reinforce when a child demonstrates good manners. For example, child A opens the door to allow all her class-mates to pass through. When the teacher passes first she thanks the child and in doing so she encourages all the other children to do the same. Child A is rewarded with praise and on returning to class was asked, 'How did it make you feel when all your class-mates thanked you for holding the door open?' This helps the child to understand the feel-good factor which she experienced, which she will be more likely to repeat again.

THE TOOLS

Good choice teddy

For younger children 'Good choice teddy' is an excellent reinforcer when a child makes the right choice regarding his behaviour. The teddy can be presented to him either during the day to sit on his table or at the end of the day so that he can take the teddy home. It is important that, when he is rewarded with the teddy, it is explained why he is receiving it, for example 'Jack, you are having the "Good choice teddy " today because you made the right choice and tidied up at the end of the lesson.' For more examples on how to use the 'Good choice teddy', go to the Resources section.

Good manners

Use the STEP approach to reinforce and demonstrate good manners.

- Sorry
- Thank you
- Excuse me
- Please

Raffle tickets

Rewarding good behaviour with raffle tickets is a great motivator for children of all ages. Children experience the 'feel-good factor' knowing that the more raffle tickets they receive the greater the chance they have of winning a prize. Arrange a raffle draw at the end of the day, week or term with great prizes.

Praise wall

After the raffle draw compress the raffle tickets into a brick using a recycling brick maker. Once the bricks have dried out, paint them a bright colour and write a positive message on each one. Over time you will create for yourself a positive wall in your class for everyone to see.

Stickers

These are a convenient way to reward children. Giving a child too many stickers will reduce their value, therefore be specific when giving a sticker so that the child feels a real sense of achievement. Stickers are available on the internet and can be personalised to the school and to the behaviour. Lunchtime stickers are great rewards to promote good lunchtime behaviour.

Reward table

Set up an area in the classroom where children can go and enjoy a fun activity, for example Lego, making play dough, painting. Use this area as a reward table and if children follow class rules they can be selected to spend five to ten minutes enjoying the activity. If available use an egg timer so that the children can use the area independently and notify the next children to be rewarded.

Certificates

These are a great way to reward children and reinforcing the behaviour you want to see, for example, good listening. When giving a child a certificate make sure it is a class celebration. Children love certificates which are sent home to parents or carers to show that their good behaviour has been rewarded in school.

Friday fun

It is always good to reward those children who have made the right choices with an end-of-week reward. Discuss with your class the type of rewards they would like to have, for example, face painting, making jewellery, playing bingo, outdoor games. To keep the motivation change the reward weekly.

Phone call/note home

A simple phone call or note home to the child's parent(s)/carer(s) is a very powerful positive reinforcer. Very often letters are sent home to give a negative message. It's lovely to send out a positive message on school headed paper. Children get very excited waiting for the post to arrive!

Special Day

Special Day provides a positive start to each day and an ideal way to reinforce all the positive behavioural changes each child has made. Imagine having 10–30 children in the class saying something positive about one child; the effect is amazing in boosting self-esteem and, more importantly, acts as a powerful reinforcer for good behaviour. Every day a child is chosen for Special Day and stands in front of the class and in turn the children, including the teacher, say a positive comment about the child, for example, 'I like Elli because she plays with me when I'm on my own in the playground.' The child whose special day it is has a series of privileges for the day, for example, being first in the queue for lunch.

Ask me why I've been good

When a child has demonstrated positive behaviour, for example, by helping her friend, she can wear a medallion around her neck. On the medallion is written 'Ask me why I've been good'; this encourages staff and pupils to ask the child and in doing so helps to reinforce her positive behaviour. A medallion can be made very simply by using a blank CD and threading a piece of ribbon through the centre. A personal message can be written on each one with a permanent marker pen. Once finished with they can either be sent home or displayed as a mobile in the classroom.

Secret student

Every day one child is secretly chosen by the teacher as a secret student; the key to this activity is that the children do not know who the secret student is, therefore everyone must behave well. To ensure all children have the chance of being the secret student, put all names in a hat and randomly choose one a day. In the morning during registration the teacher tells the class that the secret student has been chosen and if they achieve, for example, ten positives by the end of the day, the whole class will be rewarded and the secret student's identity is revealed (if the class do not achieve the set goal then the student's identity is not revealed).

Fuel the rocket!

In groups, give the children a transparent long tube and ask them to design a rocket using the tube; for example, the wings of the rocket would go on the side of the tubing. Display the rockets either on a wall or on a table with the names of the children underneath each rocket. When the group displays a positive behaviour or achieves a task drop a red plastic disc into the rocket. When the group's tube is full of fuel and ready to launch, reward the group, for example, with free time.

All children like to be rewarded, and every time a child makes the right choices we will have a school we can all be proud of if we can celebrate this achievement! If the achievement is shared with the whole school, everybody benefits. One easy and quick way of doing this is by splitting the school up into house teams. Each child is rewarded individually and given a token or point, which is put forward into a house team point system. At the end of the week, each class or year group adds up their tokens or points and these are then collated throughout the whole school. School assemblies are an ideal way to share house team achievements.

Activity ticket

Ask the children to list all the activities they'd like to do in school as a special reward, for example, time on a laptop, a game of baseball, painting, having dinner with the headteacher. These activities can then be made into prizes. Ask the children to design an 'Activity Ticket' which they collect for all positive behaviour seen by staff. Decide on the number of tickets required for each activity; when a child collects the required number of tickets she can then be rewarded with that activity.

The safe

This is a brilliant way to motivate individual children. A child is given a money-box safe with a combination lock. Explain to her that if she collects X amount of points she will receive a main reward towards the end of the day. Place the safe away from the children so that it does not cause distraction. When she displays appropriate behaviours, however small, reward her with a white counter to place in her locked safe. A white counter is worth one point. If she displays inappropriate behaviour the teacher will place a red counter in her safe. This red counter cancels out a white counter. If the child displays appropriate behaviour at the end of the day she is given the combination to the safe, and she must count how many white counters she has and subtract any red counters.

Free time

Giving 'free time' is a great reward to give to a child, for example, when she has completed a piece of work. It keeps her focused and on-task knowing that she can have time to choose her own activity.

Photo gallery

They say that a picture is worth a thousand words, so imagine the impact created by displaying a photo gallery in the classroom of all the rewards, activities, trips, etc. the children have experienced through demonstrating good behaviour. This not only helps to reinforce the children's achievements, but also gives them a clear vision of change, confidence and a feeling of wellbeing. Children who see themselves on view feel loved, valued and special. This also provides an excellent reinforcer for a child who has engaged in difficult behaviour to take time to look at the photos to remind her what she has already achieved.

Friday trophy

Reward a child with the class trophy at the end of the week, for example, for being consistent in handing in her homework. The child can take the trophy home for the weekend and keep it on her desk for the rest of the week. To ensure all the children at some time during the year receive the trophy keep a whole-class tick list.

Feeding time at the zoo

In groups, ask the children to choose an animal, for example, a giraffe. Draw and colour the animal's head and stick it on top of a transparent long tube then attach it to a wall in the classroom. When the group displays a positive behaviour, or achieves a task, drop a plastic ping pong ball into the animal's mouth. When the group's tube is full, reward, for example, with free time.

PART II

POSITIVE CLASSROOM MANAGEMENT

We both firmly believe that every single child deserves to be given a chance in life irrespective of his social, economic and emotional status. This can only be done if classrooms are positive and when teachers allow children to take ownership and responsibility for themselves. Encouraging children to make the right choices and praising them when they do is a real step in the right direction.

If we think of the classroom as a large jigsaw, then a single piece of jigsaw represents an individual child. For the picture to look complete every single piece needs to be put carefully in the right place. This will only happen if we have the correct expertise to know how to do it and that we give it the right time and attention. It only takes one piece to be put in the wrong place for the picture to be disunited! It is this harmonious picture that we are seeking to create.

Is your teaching effective?

We do have a responsibility as teachers to provide children with a curriculum which is stimulating and which promotes inquisitive, independent thinking. Daily lessons which engage and encourage children to take ownership of their learning are those lessons which, from our experience, have the least behaviour problems. Children enjoy learning, and the more creative and imaginative lessons we create the more learning becomes fun!

A two-year research report that focused on effective classroom practice was undertaken between 2006 and 2008, led by Professor Day and a team at the University of Nottingham (Day *et al.* 2008). The report aimed to draw out the key factors that contribute to effective teaching.

Eighty teachers were recruited from schools identified as being effective, based on examination and assessment data. The research considered the learning environment, the lessons themselves and teacher personality. Findings showed that the more effective teachers create a positive climate for learning by challenging children's ideas, inspiring them, being more innovative in their practice and differentiating among children according to their abilities and interests where appropriate. The report clearly showed that it is not necessarily the teachers with the most experience who are the most effective. The following qualities were seen in the most effective teaching:

- enthusiasm for their work

- high aspirations for the success of every child

- positive relationships

- high motivation

- commitment and resilience

- good subject knowledge

- enthusiasm for their work

- high aspirations for the success of every child

- positive relationships

- high motivation

- commitment and resilience

- good subject knowledge.

With these qualities the most effective teachers are able to focus on building self-esteem, engendering trust and maintaining respect. If you are showing and demonstrating these qualities in your classroom you can be confident that your classroom is a positive learning environment.

Tool 6

Establishing Effective Routines

The behaviour

Routines help to minimise behavioural challenges in the classroom and are key to a well-managed and organised classroom. Pupils enjoy routines, which are easy to understand and easy to accomplish, yet flexible enough to alter if circumstances change. Research shows that most behavioural problems result from a lack of consistent classroom routines. Successful classrooms have routines for the following:

- meeting and greeting children and visitors entering the classroom

- successful transitions into the class

- moving around the classroom

- registration

- strategic seating

- lateness

- getting the children's attention

- finishing work early

- pencil sharpening

- asking for assistance

- break time and lunchtime

- handing out equipment

- homework
- going to the toilet
- class jobs
- fire drill
- tidying up
- successful transitions leaving the classroom
- home time.

THE TOOLS
Establishing routines

Display the class routines and go over them with the pupils on a regular basis. Check pupils' understanding of the routines. Explain the rationale behind the routine. Model the routine or procedure for the pupils. Be consistent. Take time re-enforcing the routines because when they are established at the beginning of the year, the entire rest of the year will be more enjoyable and productive for both teacher and pupils.

Pupil voice

It is important to include the children in your class when creating routines as this gives them ownership and they'll be more likely to reinforce them. The more involved children are in routines the smoother your class will run.

Do we need a routine?

At the beginning of the school year ask the class in groups to think about routines, why the class should have routines. Then get the children to identify problems or potential problems within the classroom which can be solved by putting in routines. When these problems or hotspots have been identified get the children to think of fun activities which can be used as routines, for example, playing *Mission Impossible* music when it's time to tidy up.

Symbols

Children sometimes need to be prompted regarding routines; a great way to do this is through symbols. Have the children photograph or draw the routines, laminate them and place each of them in the designated area of the classroom to remind the children, for example, hanging up coats. When it is time for the children to carry out the routine the teacher can just point to the symbol.

Self registration

A great way to start the day is for children to help with registration. Turn it into a game: when their names are called out, ask them each to answer with a description of how they feel that morning, for example, happy, excited, tired. Encourage individual children to respond in a foreign language or use a number system. Each child is given a number and acknowledges her attendance by saying her given number. This is a quick and fun way of taking registration. Electronic registration is also a quick and easy way of registering children.

Routine to the beat

A fun way to reinforce routines is to use music. Using music from TV shows or films can be used to signal when the class need to tidy up at the end of the lesson. The length of the music is important as the class need to know how long they've got; for example, to tidy up, the *Mission Impossible* theme music is great for this. The use of IT to reinforce routines is visual and fun. Websites which show countdown clocks and egg-timers are great resources for the class.

Handing out equipment

Choose children in the class to be responsible for handing out equipment at the beginning of the lesson to limit unnecessary disruption. Change the group of children every half term.

Asking for assistance

Signal flaps

Laminate three coloured strips of paper, red, orange and green, and stick them to the front of the child's desk. If the child doesn't need assistance she flips the green strip, if she's not too sure of the task she flips the orange strip and if she needs assistance she flips the red strip.

Traffic light cups

Similar to the 'Signal flaps' each child has a red, orange and green cup. She displays the appropriate coloured cup to show you her level of understanding. A green cup shows that she has understood the task, an orange cup shows that she has understood some of the concept and a red cup means that she has not understood at all and needs some further level of assistance.

Tool 7

Helping the Children to Enter the Classroom Successfully

The behaviour

We never know when children enter our classrooms exactly what emotions they may be carrying with them before school actually starts. Ultimately, we want every single child to be happy and excited about coming into the classroom with a real thirst for learning. In reality this is more difficult for some children than others. As the teacher we need to create a warm, personal, caring yet firm approach to establish the expectations that are required to create a positive learning environment. Children need to be motivated to learn and entering the classroom with a positive attitude is a great way to start the day!

THE TOOLS

Meet and greet

Everyone wants to feel valued and special, and this includes children. We never know what sort of morning they have had before they come to school, therefore the way we meet and greet them is essential in order to make them feel valued, as well as to communicate the class' expectations, rules and routines. Letting them know what we expect them to do when they enter the classroom is vital, otherwise they could engage in unwanted behaviour.

In order to do this we need (even on our off days) to convince them that this is where we want to be because they are important. Standing at the door with a welcoming smile and engaging them in conversation, for example, 'How did you enjoy your trip to the cinema with Mum yesterday?', shows that we are interested in them and their lives.

Is there a problem?

If a child is not happy when he arrives at school in the morning then invest some time into establishing what the problem is. Just listening to him can eliminate potential unwanted behaviour from taking place. The problem could be, for example, that he didn't have any breakfast which can be addressed by giving him a slice of toast or piece of fruit.

Successful transitions into the classroom

First contact

It is essential that your first contact with the children is a welcoming one. You need to establish respect immediately in a calm, assertive manner and communicate that the classroom has set rules and expectations. A useful technique is to greet the children outside your classroom, by standing at the door and welcoming them in. Be in place ready for them as they arrive. The children must enter the classroom in an orderly fashion sitting at their desks and completing a task which you have previously prepared. Remember positively to reinforce good behaviour with praise.

Not ready to come into my classroom?

It is highly likely that one or two (or maybe more!) children will 'test' boundaries, and will not enter the classroom as you want them to; for example, they may start talking or shouting out, or trying to jump the queue. A very useful strategy to manage this is very promptly and assertively to say to the child, 'You're not ready to come into the classroom...please wait there until you are ready to come in.'

Return to the child whom you have asked to wait outside the classroom, and say to him, 'Are you now ready to come into the classroom?' It is highly likely that the child will now be ready and will enter the classroom in a calm and focused manner.

Positively reinforce

Once all the other children are sitting in the classroom, prompt them again on the set task and praise those who are completing the task well. Also hand out token rewards (see Rewards section). Say, 'Well done child A for reading quietly. I wonder who else I can see reading quietly?' This way the children are more motivated to carry out the task in order to receive the reward.

The class is now calm and focused and ready for the first lesson to be introduced. Repeat this process every time the children enter the classroom throughout the day. The children then know what is expected of them.

Reflection time

Relaxation tracks

Just before the first lesson of the day prepare the children by playing a short one- to three-minute relaxation track. Encourage them to sit with their eyes closed or with their heads in their hands to help them focus. After the relaxation track the children will be calm and ready to begin the school day. This can be repeated after first break time and the lunchtime break to help refocus the children so that they are calm and ready to engage and learn. There are some useful contacts in the resource list at the back of the book.

Peer massage

Providing the school has been trained in delivering peer massage, this is a great way to help to calm and help improve the children's concentration. Peer massage has many more benefits; these include:

- developing respect for one another
- reducing bullying and aggression
- helping to settle and focus the children in school
- building positive relationships
- increasing self-esteem and confidence
- helping children understand safe touch.

Tool 8

Addressing Lateness

The behaviour

Children arriving to class late can be a common problem. There are many reasons why a child maybe late for school:

- problems with transport
- bullying on the way to school
- vulnerable groups, for example traveller children
- emotional problems
- difficulties at home.

SELF-ASSESSMENT CHECKLIST

As teachers we are constantly faced with challenges every day and providing solutions to these challenges is not an easy task. Sometimes, however hard we try, certain situations push our professionalism to the limit. When this happens we need to take a deep breath and ask ourselves some basic questions as to why these things are happening.

Here is a simple five-step checklist to do a quick self-assessment for any situation which you may face in the classroom. If you can answer all these questions then you know that you have got the basics covered and can go ahead with finding the right tool to fit the right behaviour. Spending a short time doing this before you implement the tool will ensure that you achieve ultimate success.

Step 1 Check the history

Play detective and find out all you can about the behaviour and the child. It may mean finding out what her behaviour was like the previous year, meeting with her class teacher or phoning up her previous school. Gather as much information as you can. What strategies were previously used? Was there parental involvement? Attendance record? Friendship groups? Academic performance?

Step 2 Check by establishing the 'Why?'

There is always a reason behind every behaviour. Behaviour is a form of communication; sometimes children (and adults) find it difficult to communicate how they are feeling because they don't know what words to use and find it easier to act out the way they feel which can sometimes result in unwanted behaviour. This behaviour is an indication that something is not right and/or their needs are not being met.

By observing and talking to the child and, if appropriate, to her parent(s)/carer(s), you can start to piece together the 'behaviour jigsaw puzzle' in order to create the big picture and establish why she is behaving in this way. When the 'why?' has been established you can then help her to understand and manage that behaviour.

Step 3 Check positive reinforcement

Make sure that the child knows that you care about her. Remember that she may have taken a long time to develop this behaviour, so be consistent and patient as the behaviour takes time to change. Establishing a good relationship with a child shows that you are interested in her and promotes her self-esteem. Remember that behaviours occur for a reason and children who display challenging behaviour do not have the skills that adults have in dealing with situations. Are you using positive language? Are your positive reinforcements exciting and motivational? Do your rewards excite and motivate children? Are you consistent in your approach?

Step 4 Check class rules

Rules create clear expectations for children and define what is acceptable behaviour. Are your class rules clear and do all the children in the class understand and respect them? Are they brightly and prominently displayed, and reinforced on a regular basis?

Step 5 Check correctives

Are you consistent in your approach to implementing your correctives within the classroom? Do children see this as fair? Children usually respect fair play. Are your correctives fair, consistent and a logical and realistic response to the behaviour?

THE TOOLS

Keep the flow

When children arrive late to class they can disrupt the flow of the lesson by, for example, trying to ask you what they need to do. This can be minimised by setting out a procedure for lateness which can involve acknowledging the child as she enters the room and directing her to complete pre-prepared work until you are ready to explain the current activity to her.

Follow up

The reason for a child's lateness must always be followed up in compliance with the school's policy. If necessary a meeting with her parent(s)/carer(s) is also advisable as her lateness may not be her fault. It is important that the class see you dealing with the lateness and following through with the school's set procedure.

Team tables

If lateness is a problem in your class consider putting the children into teams. These teams can score points, for example, making sensible choices, completing work, arriving to class on time. This form of peer pressure is very effective and it also motivates the children to arrive to class on time. Give the teams a goal and reward them with an end-of-week, -month, -term reward.

Buddy-up

Encourage the children to buddy-up with another child from school who lives close to them so that they can walk to school together. This is effective as both children have a responsibility to each other to arrive to school on time.

Model the behaviour

Modelling the behaviour you want to see is very effective when encouraging the children to make the right choices. If you arrive late to the classroom, then what message is that sending to the children? Always arrive in class on time ready to greet the children.

Walking bus service

Set up a walking bus service in school to support parents who find it difficult to get children to school on time. This way parking congestion outside the school gates is avoided and children get to observe their local environment. A service of this kind needs to be properly supervised and the correct risk assessments need to be carried out. It can be a very successful way of supporting parents and children to arrive at school at the correct time.

Bibliotherapy

To help children understand and learn to manage their feelings introduce them to a range of books, for example, about being late. Children sometimes find it easy to relate to characters in a book and this in itself can help them understand their own problem(s) and develop coping strategies.

The next step

When the behaviour has been identified and a tool has been tried and implemented you may find the behaviour is still being displayed. Here are some suggestions for the next step.

Step 1 Arrange a meeting with the parent(s)/carer(s) to discuss the behaviour and the way forward.

Step 2 Meet with the Special Educational Needs Co-ordinator (SENCO), or equivalent outside the UK, and discuss the possibility of devising an individual behaviour plan with specific measurable targets.

Step 3 Give time for the behaviour to change. Small steps make the biggest changes.

Step 4 Remember that all children are different and one tool does not fit all. Try a variety of different tools to find the best tool for you and your class.

Tool 9

Achieving Successful Lessons

The behaviour

The most successful lessons excite, empower and engage children. Teachers who plan creative and imaginative lessons are rewarded with children who are attentive, on-task and have the fewest displays of unwanted behaviour. Thorough planning and good organisation strategies will support you in delivering the type of lessons you wish to teach. If you are at the end of your tether and exhausted all the techniques that you know, then why not have a go at the following tools? They may surprise you!

THE TOOLS

Strategic seating

Always sit children who have the potential to display unwanted behaviour, or have difficulty concentrating, facing towards the teacher. This way, the teacher is able to 'catch' both good and difficult behaviour early, for example, eyes wandering, facial expressions. When a child begins to display inappropriate behaviours, however small, immediately catch the behaviour before it escalates to a level where it becomes too difficult to control.

Seating plan

Seating plans and layouts in classrooms can vary tremendously. According to the British Council teachers should consider the following when seating children:

- Can I see childrens' faces? Can they see me?
- Can everyone see the board (if you're planning on using it)?
- Can the children see one another?
- Can I move around the room so that I can monitor effectively?

Map out the classroom and allocate each child a place at a table and on the carpet. This eliminates unwanted behaviour, arguments regarding who's sitting next to whom and also avoids a stampede to get to their favourite places on the carpet especially if there are soft furnishings for them to sit on.

Seating by cards

To randomly seat the children in class give each child a playing card. This way the children can be seated according to suit, for example hearts, clubs or by odds (3, 5, 7) or evens (2, 4, 6).

The lesson

Gaining the children's attention before starting a lesson is essential in order to create a positive learning environment.

Getting their attention

When ready to start the lesson wait until you have the children's full attention (see Tool 14, Getting the children's attention). It is very important not to start to speak to the class if any of the children are still talking.

The task

Explain the task and check the children's understanding. Structure lessons into short sessions to help maintain the children's attention. Ensure that the input time is short and to the point; keep to the rule of one minute for each year of the child's age, for example if the majority of the children in the class are eight years old then the input should last no longer than eight minutes.

Differentiation

Unwanted behaviour can sometimes develop if we have not planned to meet the needs of children. Differentiating work for all abilities is essential for children to achieve what is expected of them. Hands-on practical resources to support the less able will clarify understanding and help the children stay on-task. Children who are off-task become distracted and begin to display attention-seeking behaviours. It is also important to plan challenge into lessons so that children are constantly stimulated and interest is sustained.

Partner time

There may be opportunities during the lesson for the children to work with a partner. To eliminate disagreements and any other unwanted behaviour from taking place give each child a picture of a clock then ask him to write the names of the friends with whom he'd like to work next to a number on the clock; for example, John Moore: 1 o'clock. When it's time for the children to work with a partner you call out a time on the clock and the child works with that friend, for example, 9 o'clock: Ahmad Ali.

Position of the teacher

The position of the teacher in the classroom is key to establishing a positive learning atmosphere. If possible try not to stand or sit with your back to the children to enable you to identify appropriate and inappropriate behaviours immediately and respond appropriately. When using a board, write at an angle in order to have a full view of the classroom. Establish the whole room as your territory by moving around. Scan the classroom, and 'sweep' it with your eyes over and over to 'catch' appropriate or inappropriate behaviour.

End of the lesson

At the end of the lesson inform the children that there will be a competition in the form of a table inspection. They will have, for example, 60 seconds to tidy their work areas and a mark out of ten will be allocated to each table.

Inform the class what went well with the lesson and thank them for their participation.

Stand at the door and dismiss the children in small groups to prevent congestion in the corridor.

As each child is dismissed, either say something positive to him or give him a smile and say, 'Goodbye'.

Noise level

Partner voices

If the lesson requires quiet partner talking, one way to ensure this is happening is to catch a child whispering as soon as the activity has been set. Stop the class and reward that child for whispering with a token reward. Whispering starts to become contagious and by rewarding certain children throughout the lesson, you'll find that the whole class is concentrating on the activity in a quiet and productive atmosphere. Children soon begin to associate different voice levels with certain activities.

Can you hear the music?

This is an effective way to maintain a certain noise level in the classroom. If the noise level becomes too high the music cannot be heard, therefore when this happens the teacher asks the children, 'Can you hear the music?' The children must lower their voices so that the music can be heard. Adjust the volume of music if the class is to work in silence, partner voices or group discussions.

Tidy-up time

Hidden in the mess

Tidying-up time can be fun; whatever the class theme is include it in the tidying-up process. Inform the children that there are, for example, spheres hidden in the mess around the classroom; for every sphere the children find they get a reward token. Only when the classroom is tidied should you end the game and announce the winners.

Tidy up to the beat

Choose a piece of music which will be synonymous with tidying up. When the music is played ask the children to tidy up to the beat of the music, encourage them to dance around the classroom and at the same time, for example, put their books away. When the class is tidy stop the music.

Busy bees

Design a 2D beehive and place it on a wall in your classroom; cut out a bee for every child. Ask the children to write their names on their bees. Place all the bees on the beehive, then select the bees of all children who have been assigned a job and place them around the beehive. When it's tidy-up time ask the busy bees (those around the beehive) to carry out their jobs. Rotate the job assignment every week or month.

Tool 10

Stopping Unwanted Behaviour during Assembly

The behaviour

It is a statutory requirement in the UK that every single child, unless for religious reasons, attends a daily act of collective worship. Assembly time is a time for spiritual reflection and moral teaching. Creating a sense of belonging to a school community through prayer, song and story is an important way of creating this reflection time with one another. To achieve this we need to encourage children to be calm and good listeners and to think about how their behaviour may influence others.,

SELF-ASSESSMENT CHECKLIST

As teachers we are constantly faced with challenges every day and providing solutions to these challenges is not an easy task. Sometimes, however hard we try, certain situations push our professionalism to the limit. When this happens we need to take a deep breath and ask ourselves some basic questions as to why these things are happening.

Here is a simple five-step checklist to do a quick self-assessment for any situation which you may face in the classroom. If you can answer all these questions then you know that you have got the basics covered and can go ahead with finding the right tool to fit the right behaviour. Spending a short time doing this before you implement the tool will ensure that you achieve ultimate success.

Step 1 Check the history

Play detective and find out all you can about the behaviour and the child. It may mean finding out what her behaviour was like the previous year, meeting with her class teacher or phoning up her previous school. Gather as much information as you can. What strategies were previously used? Was there parental involvement? Attendance record? Friendship groups? Academic performance?

Step 2 Check by establishing the 'Why?'

There is always a reason behind every behaviour. Behaviour is a form of communication; sometimes children (and adults) find it difficult to communicate how they are feeling because they don't know what words to use and find it easier to act out the way they feel which can sometimes result in unwanted behaviour. This behaviour is an indication that something is not right and/or their needs are not being met.

By observing and talking to the child and, if appropriate, to her parent(s)/carer(s) you can start to piece together the 'behaviour jigsaw puzzle' in order to create the big picture and establish why she is behaving in this way. When the 'why?' has been established you can then help her to understand and manage that behaviour.

Step 3 Check positive reinforcement

Make sure that the child knows that you care about her. Remember that she may have taken a long time to develop this behaviour, so be consistent and patient as the behaviour takes time to change. Establishing a good relationship with a child shows that you are interested in her and promotes her self-esteem. Remember that behaviours occur for a reason and children who display challenging behaviour do not have the skills that adults have in dealing with situations. Are you using positive language? Are your positive reinforcements exciting and motivational? Do your rewards excite and motivate children? Are you consistent in your approach?

Step 4 Check class rules

Rules create clear expectations for children and define what is acceptable behaviour. Are your class rules clear and do all the children in the class understand and respect them? Are they brightly and prominently displayed, and reinforced on a regular basis?

Step 5 Check correctives

Are you consistent in your approach to implementing your correctives within the classroom? Do children see this as fair? Children usually respect fair play. Are your correctives fair, consistent and a logical and realistic response to the behaviour?

THE TOOLS

Role model

How can we possibly expect children to be calm and attentive during assembly if teachers do not role model the expectations themselves? By sitting calmly and not talking and chatting to others you are showing your class the type of behaviour that you want them to display.

Getting ready for assembly

Line the children up in assembly order making sure that children who have the potential to disrupt have been positioned strategically in the line so that they are in between children who are unlikely to display unwanted behaviour. Having a calm relaxation time before going into assembly will help prepare your class for the forthcoming assembly. Children should leave the classroom calmly and without a lot of noise and disruption. This can be practised and does work!

Walking into assembly

It is highly likely that one or two (or maybe more!) children will 'test' boundaries, and will not enter the hall as you want them to; for example, they may start talking or shouting out, or trying to jump the queue. A very useful strategy to manage this is to very promptly and assertively say to the child, 'You're not ready to come into the hall...please wait there until you are ready to come in.'

Return to the child whom you have asked to wait outside the hall, and say to him, 'Are you now ready to come into the hall?' It is highly likely that the child will now be ready and will enter the hall in a calm and focused manner.

Seating in assembly

If the children come into assembly in order (see 'Getting ready for assembly'), then the potential for unwanted behaviour taking place while seated will be greatly reduced.

Position of the teacher

The position of the teacher during assembly is key to establishing a reflective and engaging atmosphere. Position yourself with your class near any child who could display unwanted behaviour. Proximity is a very powerful tool to help deter unwanted behaviour. Scan your class and 'sweep' them with your eyes over and over to 'catch' appropriate or inappropriate behaviour.

Non-verbal communication

If a child is displaying unwanted behaviour communicate your expectations non-verbally, for example, putting your finger to your lips to signal no talking. Sometimes all children need is a gentle reminder to help them re-engage. If a child's behaviour becomes disruptive then follow your class correctives. Just as important is positively reinforcing the behaviour you want to see by giving a child a thumbs-up or a smile.

Top jobs

If you have a child in your class who finds it difficult to display the right behaviour during assembly then assign him a job, for example, operating the projector. This not only re-directs his attention but can also boost his self-esteem by giving him a position of responsibility.

Team houses

Encourage children to display the right behaviour during assembly by putting them in their house teams. These house teams can score points for good behaviour during assembly. This form of peer pressure is very effective. Give the house teams a goal and reward them with an end-of-day, end-of-week, -month, -term reward.

Reward chart

If a child is likely to display unwanted behaviour during assembly then set him achievable goals to help him to make the right choices. These goals can be set via a reward chart. Reward charts can be used to manage a classroom community or modify the behaviour of a single child. They are an effective way to motivate a child as he can track his own progress, providing that he understands what is meant by good behaviour and can stay focused until he achieves the overall reward, i.e. at the end of a lesson, day or week. Decide the goals with the child, for example to walk into assembly, sit sensibly for five minutes with the class, then, under supervision, complete a task in another room. Once the child has achieved this goal extend the time, for example, to ten minutes and so on.

Bibliotherapy

To help children understand and learn to manage their feelings introduce them to a range of books, for example, about feeling angry. Children sometimes find it easy to relate to characters in a book and this in itself can help them to understand their own problem(s) and develop coping strategies.

The next step

When the behaviour has been identified and a tool has been tried and implemented you may find the behaviour is still being displayed. Here are some suggestions for the next step.

Step 1 Arrange a meeting with the parent(s)/carer(s) to discuss the behaviour and the way forward.

Step 2 Meet with the Special Educational Needs Co-ordinator (SENCO), or equivalent outside the UK, and discuss the possibility of devising an individual behaviour plan with specific measurable targets.

Step 3 Give time for the behaviour to change. Small steps make the biggest changes.

Step 4 Remember that all children are different and one tool does not fit all. Try a variety of different tools to find the best tool for you and your class.

Tool 11

Preventing Children from Leaving the Classroom without Permission

The behaviour

For a child to leave the class without permission is not only unacceptable but it could also result in a child putting herself at risk.

Possible reasons for leaving the classroom without permission:

- lack of rules and boundaries

- trying to gain the teacher's attention

- upset by something going on in the class

- a desire to go somewhere more appealing

- a reaction to something they find challenging

- find a task too difficult to complete.

SELF-ASSESSMENT CHECKLIST

As teachers we are constantly faced with challenges every day and providing solutions to these challenges is not an easy task. Sometimes, however hard we try, certain situations push our professionalism to the limit. When this happens we need to take a deep breath and ask ourselves some basic questions as to why these things are happening.

Here is a simple five-step checklist to do a quick self-assessment for any situation which you may face in the classroom. If you can answer all these questions then you know that you have got the basics covered and can go ahead with finding the right tool to fit the right behaviour. Spending a short time doing this before you implement the tool will ensure that you achieve ultimate success.

Step 1 Check the history

Play detective and find out all you can about the behaviour and the child. It may mean finding out what her behaviour was like the previous year, meeting with her class teacher or phoning up her previous school. Gather as much information as you can. What strategies were previously used? Was there parental involvement? Attendance record? Friendship groups? Academic performance?

Step 2 Check by establishing the 'Why?'

There is always a reason behind every behaviour. Behaviour is a form of communication; sometimes children (and adults) find it difficult to communicate how they are feeling because they don't know what words to use and find it easier to act out the way they feel which can sometimes result in unwanted behaviour. This behaviour is an indication that something is not right and/or their needs are not being met.

By observing and talking to the child and, if appropriate, to her parent(s)/carer(s), you can start to piece together the 'behaviour jigsaw puzzle' in order to create the big picture and establish why she is behaving in this way. When the 'why?' has been established you can then help her to understand and manage that behaviour.

Step 3 Check positive reinforcement

Make sure the child knows you care about her. Remember that she may have taken a long time to develop this behaviour, so be consistent and patient as the behaviour takes time to change.

Establishing a good relationship with a child shows that you are interested in her and promotes her self-esteem. Remember that behaviours occur for a reason and children who display challenging behaviour do not have the skills that adults have in dealing with situations. Are you using positive language? Are your positive reinforcements exciting and motivational? Do your rewards excite and motivate children? Are you consistent in your approach?

Step 4 Check class rules

Rules create clear expectations for children and define what is acceptable behaviour. Are your class rules clear and do all the children in the class understand and respect them? Are they brightly and prominently displayed, and reinforced on a regular basis?

Step 5 Check correctives

Are you consistent in your approach to implementing your correctives within the classroom? Do children see this as fair? Children usually respect fair play. Are your correctives fair, consistent and a logical and realistic response to the behaviour?

THE TOOLS

Immediate response

Regardless of why a child has left the classroom without permission, her whereabouts must be established immediately. This can be achieved by informing the headteacher, a member of the senior management team (SMT) or the office staff.

The approach taken to help the child positively manage her behaviour depends on her reason for leaving the class. Here are a few suggestions:

Cat and mouse

Don't chase after a child as this results in a 'cat and mouse'-type game creating an unwanted high-energy reaction to the behaviour. This will not only encourage her to leave the classroom again without permission but it could also put you and the child in danger, for example, by running across the car park or onto a main road.

Stay calm

Before dealing with the situation make sure you're calm and relaxed; this is important as it will not only help the child but will also ensure that the situation is dealt with in a consistent and fair way.

Attention-seeking behaviour

If the child leaves the classroom because she is trying to gain the teacher's attention, have minimal interaction with her when she is returned to the class and involve her in the class task. The reason for this is to avoid letting her believe that the way to get attention is to leave the room.

Quiet time card

Provide the child with a 'quiet time' card which she can show when she feels that she wants to leave the classroom. This card allows her five to ten minutes of quiet time either within the classroom or within a partner classroom. When she shows the card she is rewarded for making the right choice instead of leaving the room without permission.

Going to the toilet

If the child is leaving the classroom without permission to go to the toilet see Tool 12 'Dealing with issues around going to the toilet'.

Bibliotherapy

To help children understand and learn to manage their feelings introduce them to a range of books, for example, about feeling upset. Children sometimes find it easy to relate to characters in a book and this in itself can help them to understand their own problem(s) and to develop coping strategies.

The next step

When the behaviour has been identified and a tool has been tried and implemented you may find the behaviour is still being displayed. Here are some suggestions for the next step.

Step 1 Arrange a meeting with the parent(s)/carer(s) to discuss the behaviour and the way forward.

Step 2 Meet with the Special Educational Needs Co-ordinator (SENCO), or equivalent in the UK, and discuss the possibility of devising an individual behaviour plan with specific measurable targets.

Step 3 Give time for the behaviour to change. Small steps make the biggest changes.

Step 4 Remember that all children are different and one tool does not fit all. Try a variety of different tools to find the best tool for you and your class.

Tool 12

Dealing with Issues around Going to the Toilet

The behaviour

Children's toilets can be a vulnerable place within a school as they are generally unsupervised particularly during lesson time. Bullying, time wasting, graffiti on walls, damage to property and flooding are all behaviours which can be common in schools. If we are proactive there are strategies which can be applied to avoid these behaviours happening in the first place.

SELF-ASSESSMENT CHECKLIST

As teachers we are constantly faced with challenges every day and providing solutions to these challenges is not an easy task. Sometimes, however hard we try, certain situations push our professionalism to the limit. When this happens we need to take a deep breath and ask ourselves some basic questions as to why these things are happening.

Here is a simple five-step checklist to do a quick self-assessment for any situation which you may face in the classroom. If you can answer all these questions then you know that you have got the basics covered and can go ahead with finding the right tool to fit the right behaviour. Spending a short time doing this before you implement the tool will ensure that you achieve ultimate success.

Step 1 Check the history

Play detective and find out all you can about the behaviour and the child. It may mean finding out what her behaviour was like the previous year, meeting with her class teacher or phoning up her previous school. Gather as much information as you can. What strategies were previously used? Was there parental involvement? Attendance record? Friendship groups? Academic performance?

Step 2 Check by establishing the 'Why?'

There is always a reason behind every behaviour. Behaviour is a form of communication; sometimes children (and adults) find it difficult to communicate how they are feeling because they don't know what words to use and find it easier to act out the way they feel which can sometimes result in unwanted behaviour. This behaviour is an indication that something is not right and/or their needs are not being met.

By observing and talking to the child and, if appropriate, to her parent(s)/carer(s), you can start to piece together the 'behaviour jigsaw puzzle' in order to create the big picture and establish why she is behaving in this way. When the 'why?' has been established you can then help her to understand and manage that behaviour.

Step 3 Check positive reinforcement

Make sure that the child knows you care about her. Remember that she may have taken a long time to develop this behaviour, so be consistent and patient as the behaviour takes time to change. Establishing a good relationship with a child shows that you are interested in her and promotes her self-esteem. Remember that behaviours occur for a reason and children who display challenging behaviour do not have the skills that adults have in dealing with situations. Are you using positive language? Are your positive reinforcements exciting and motivational? Do your rewards excite and motivate children? Are you consistent in your approach?

Step 4 Check class rules

Rules create clear expectations for children and define what is acceptable behaviour. Are your class rules clear and do all the children in the class understand and respect them? Are they brightly and prominently displayed, and reinforced on a regular basis?

Step 5 Check correctives

Are you consistent in your approach to implementing your correctives within the classroom? Do children see this as fair? Children usually respect fair play. Are your correctives fair, consistent and a logical and realistic response to the behaviour?

THE TOOLS

Medical concern

If a child is frequently leaving the classroom to go to the toilet it is advisable to contact her parent/carer in case there is a medical reason, for example a urinary tract infection.

Schedule toilet breaks

Schedule set toilet breaks during the day to avoid disruption, for example:

1. before registration

2. before first break

3. before lunchtime break

4. before last break.

Monitor toilets

If someone in the classroom deliberately damages the toilets, or leaves them deliberately untidy or with graffiti on the walls, for example, establish who it is as soon as possible. This can be achieved by inspecting the toilets on a regular basis, and asking the children to write their name on a monitoring sheet every time they leave to go to the toilet. When a child has been identified an appropriate consequence must be implemented immediately and, if appropriate, a meeting with her parent(s)/carer(s).

Sign in, sign out

An effective way to monitor when and for how long each child goes to the toilet is to use a signing in, signing out sheet which can be placed by the classroom door. Next to the sheet place a clock, and the child must record the time next to her name when she leaves and when she returns to class, which gives her the opportunity to practise telling the time.

Every minute counts!

Some children tend to prolong their stay in the toilet, maybe engaging in unwanted behaviour, chatting with other children or just daydreaming. To reduce this prolonged time set an agreed time limit every time a child leaves the classroom, which can be set via a sand timer, class clock or stopwatch. Reward the child, for example, with a raffle ticket if she returns to class under the set time limit.

Toilet pass

Get the children to design a toilet pass, laminate it and attach a piece of string to it so that it can be worn easily. This can then be given to a child who wants to go to the toilet. Other members of staff can clearly see that the child has been given permission to leave the classroom and go to the toilet. The toilet pass also limits the number of children going to the toilet at any one time: before another child can go to the toilet she must wait until the pass has been returned to the classroom.

Toilet tickets

Every child is given a set number of toilet tickets per week. These tickets can be used to go to the toilet during unscheduled times. Children who visit the toilet more frequently than normal may need to seek medical advice.

Hand sanitiser pass

Hygiene is very important especially when going to the toilet. To ensure only one child goes to the toilet at any one time she takes the hand sanitiser bottle off your desk and places it on her desk; this indicates she is leaving for the toilet. On her return the child sanitises her hands and places the bottle back on your desk.

Sign it!

Children asking to go to the toilet can be disruptive to the flow of your lesson. Teaching the children the sign language for 'Please can I go to the toilet?' is not only less disruptive, but it teaches the children a new skill and it's fun.

Bibliotherapy

To help children understand and learn to manage their feelings introduce them to a range of books, for example, about feeling bored. Children sometimes find it easy to relate to characters in a book and this in itself can help them to understand their own problem(s) and develop coping strategies.

The next step

When the behaviour has been identified and a tool has been tried and implemented you may find the behaviour is still being displayed. Here are some suggestions for the next step.

> Step 1 Arrange a meeting with the parent(s)/carer(s) to discuss the behaviour and the way forward.

Step 2 Meet with the Special Educational Needs Co-ordinator (SENCO), or equivalent outside the UK, and discuss the possibility of devising an individual behaviour plan with specific measurable targets.

Step 3 Give time for the behaviour to change. Small steps make the biggest changes.

Step 4 Remember that all children are different and one tool does not fit all. Try a variety of different tools to find the best tool for you and your class.

Tool 13

Helping Children to Leave the Classroom Successfully

The behaviour

In the same way that children are encouraged to enter the classroom in a calm, positive manner it is equally as important for children to leave your classroom in the same way. Children are less likely to encounter unwanted behaviour outside the classroom if they leave with the right attitude. Whether you are taking the children for a PE lesson or into assembly, leaving the classroom calmly and sensibly will eliminate unwanted behaviour.

THE TOOLS

Expectations

Before lining up inform the children where they are going and what the expectations are, for example, 'It's time for assembly; I'll be rewarding children who line up sensibly and walk quietly into assembly.'

Lining up

If there are children who are likely to display unwanted behaviour position them strategically in the line so that they are in between children who are unlikely to display unwanted behaviour. There are a number of ways for the children to line up; here are a few:

Boy, girl, boy, girl line

To line the children up boy, girl, boy, girl ask the girls to form a line by the door, then ask the boys to line up alongside the girls by the door forming two parallel lines. When the lines are quiet ask the first boy to lead off followed by a girl, then boy, then girl. The teacher must lead by the front and if a teaching assistant is available ask them to follow the end of the line.

Alphabetical order

For older children ask them to line up in alphabetical order of their first name. Call out the letters of the alphabet and if a child's name starts with that letter he is invited to line up by the door. This lining up game can be varied, for example, by using the alphabetical order of their last names, or places of birth.

Ten hut

Line the children up in two parallel lines by the door. The teacher then gives the following instructions:

1. 'Fall out!': Children can then be messy in the line, for example, by not being in line, or by being chatty.

2. 'Ten Hut!': Children must then snap to attention by quickly putting their legs together, straightening up, with their hands by their sides, and no talking, and by being directly behind the person in front of them.

Colours

Ask the children to line up according to eye colour; for example, 'If you have hazel eyes you can line up now'.

Number up!

When the teacher has taught the class for a while and has established potential unwanted behaviours amongst the children, he can allocate a number to each child so that those children who might display unwanted behaviours are always stood next to a child who helps to promote positive behaviour. When it's lining up time the teacher calls out numbers in sequence and each child lines up respectively.

Can I hear you?

Turn it into a game; ask each table in turn to line up as quietly as they can. The other children listen to see if they can catch the other children out. Reward the quietest table.

Sign it!

Teach the children in your class their names in sign language. Then, randomly pick a name and sign it with your hands. If the respective child recognises it, he puts up his hand and is then allowed to leave the class. If he doesn't, carry on with another name until everyone has left the class. Repeat again for those children who have not understood the first time.

House teams

Line up the children according to the house to which they belong, for example green house line up first. The house that lines up quietly and sensibly is rewarded 'x' amount of house points.

Thinking game

When the children are lining up get them to think of something that begins with a certain letter. Then when the line is quiet ask each child for the word he thought of. This keeps the children occupied and less likely to behave inappropriately.

Fire drill order

Line up the children in fire drill order as it is in the class register. This is not only an effective way to line up the children but it is good practice for when there is a fire drill within the school.

Home time

WOW! vouchers

All children love praise. A great way to go home on a positive note is to give out WOW! vouchers to individual children for displaying the correct behaviour. The vouchers can easily be created on the computer. The vouchers are then filled in by the teacher and a comment made by the child before being given to his parent/carer.

WOW! Charlie has been a brilliant boy today!
I helped pick up all the toys!

Staggered dismissal

When the bell sounds to signal the end of the day, dismiss the children in small groups to avoid any unwanted behaviour. While the other groups are waiting they can be involved in a quiet activity, for example a brain-teaser.

PART III

RE-FOCUSING

Children who are not on-task, engaged in inappropriate behaviours or ignoring instructions given by the teacher are not effective learners. If these behaviours are not nipped in the bud they will very quickly affect the positive learning culture of the classroom. There are many reasons why children are not focused and we need to ensure that we have ticked all the areas of the checklist before we move on to putting in specific strategies. Sometimes, there may be a need to reinforce class expectations again with all children so that they are really clear about what is expected of them and the consequences they will receive if they do not follow them. Use words that the children will understand and be positive, focusing on what the children should be doing rather than on what they are not doing.

Children who are focused:

- understand what is expected of them
- are motivated and stimulated to complete tasks presented to them
- co-operate with others when doing paired or group work
- are good listeners
- provide good role models to others around them
- enjoy school
- involve themselves in extracurricular activities.

Tool 14

Getting the Children's Attention

The behaviour

As a class teacher it is important that when you want to get the attention of your class you are able to get them to respond to you effectively. There are many occasions when you may need to do this:

- fire drill

- an emergency within the classroom or school

- transitions within the classroom

- tidying up at the end of a lesson

- a practical lesson

- to give instructions

- starting a lesson

- breaks in the school day such as assembly time, break and lunchtime

- when the class are outside of the classroom, for example, in the school grounds or on an educational visit.

THE TOOLS

The rhythm game

1. Let the class know that when you want their attention you'll clap a rhythm and they must copy that beat. When you stop clapping this is the signal for them to look at you without talking.

2. The children who complete the task are rewarded with the chosen token reward.

3. Make it challenging for the children by clapping more complicated beats or using body percussion.

4. When increasing difficulty levels remember to provide them with challenges that they are able to complete without feeling frustrated otherwise this will have a detrimental effect on their behaviour.

Silence all around

1. Let the class know that when you want their attention you'll say '123321 silence all around has begun'; the children must then freeze with no talking.

2. The children who freeze the longest complete the task and are rewarded with the chosen token reward. If all children freeze for a set time they are all rewarded.

3. Time the children to see if they can break their best record. If they break the record they can be rewarded with extra token rewards.

Give me five

Let the class know that when you want their attention you'll hold up your hand and say, 'Give me five'. Everyone holds their hand up and begin to count down from five to one getting progressively quieter until they whisper 'one'.

Can you hear the music?

This is an effective way to maintain a certain noise level in the classroom. If the noise level becomes too high the music cannot be heard; when this happens the teacher asks the children, 'Can you hear the music?' The children must lower their voices so that the music can be heard. Adjust the volume of music depending upon whether the class is to work in silence, with partner voices or in group discussions.

Numbers to action

Pair up a number with an action, for example number one equals hands on your head, number two equals touch your toes. Then say a number or hold up your fingers to represent the number. These need to be practised with the children; new actions can be added to make the activity more interesting. Then hold up your fingers to represent the number and when the children complete the action, reward them.

The music box

Buy a traditional jewellery music box which plays music when the lid is lifted. Choose a different child every day to wind up the box. Every time you want to get the children's attention open the lid to hear the music and only close it when all the children are silent. Choose another child at the end of the day to open the box and if the music is still playing the class are rewarded as it is evident that throughout the day the class listened really well.

Tool 15

Dealing with a Lack of Motivation

The behaviour

Children who are motivated and who feel good about themselves can find handling conflicts and resisting negative pressures easier to manage. They tend to be happier, smile more and enjoy life. The way to encourage this is by rewarding the desired behaviour and in so doing motivate the child to make positive choices and enjoy positive outcomes.

Lack of motivation

There are many reasons why some children lack motivation towards school. It is important for the teacher to encourage a child to see school as a place where she can be successful. She needs to feel that she can achieve and that school is fun and interesting. It is also helpful for the teacher to understand what motivates her so that these can be used in engaging her to learn.

Possible reasons for a lack of motivation:

- low self-esteem
- learning difficulties
- poor social skills
- lack of enthusiasm
- parental influences
- victim of bullying
- lack of understanding.

SELF-ASSESSMENT CHECKLIST

As teachers we are constantly faced with challenges every day and providing solutions to these challenges is not an easy task. Sometimes, however hard we try, certain situations push our professionalism to the limit. When this happens we need to take a deep breath and ask ourselves some basic questions as to why these things are happening.

Here is a simple five-step checklist to do a quick self-assessment for any situation which you may face in the classroom. If you can answer all these questions then you know that you have got the basics covered and can go ahead with finding the right tool to fit the right behaviour. Spending a short time doing this before you implement the tool will ensure that you achieve ultimate success.

Step 1 Check the history

Play detective and find out all you can about the behaviour and the child. It may mean finding out what her behaviour was like the previous year, meeting with her class teacher or phoning up her previous school. Gather as much information as you can. What strategies were previously used? Was there parental involvement? Attendance record? Friendship groups? Academic performance?

Step 2 Check by establishing the 'Why?'

There is always a reason behind every behaviour. Behaviour is a form of communication; sometimes children (and adults) find it difficult to communicate how they are feeling because they don't know what words to use and find it easier to act out the way they feel which can sometimes result in unwanted behaviour. This behaviour is an indication that something is not right and/or their needs are not being met.

By observing and talking to the child and, if appropriate, to her parent(s)/carer(s), you can start to piece together the 'behaviour jigsaw puzzle' in order to create the big picture and

establish why she is behaving in this way. When the 'why?' has been established you can then help her to understand and manage that behaviour.

Step 3 Check positive reinforcement

Make sure that the child knows you care about her. Remember that she may have taken a long time to develop this behaviour, so be consistent and patient as the behaviour takes time to change. Establishing a good relationship with a child shows that you are interested in her and promotes her self-esteem. Remember that behaviours occur for a reason and children who display challenging behaviour do not have the skills that adults have in dealing with situations. Are you using positive language? Are your positive reinforcements exciting and motivational? Do your rewards excite and motivate children? Are you consistent in your approach?

Step 4 Check class rules

Rules create clear expectations for children and define what is acceptable behaviour. Are your class rules clear and do all the children in the class understand and respect them? Are they brightly and prominently displayed, and reinforced on a regular basis?

Step 5 Check correctives

Are you consistent in your approach to implementing your correctives within the classroom? Do children see this as fair? Children usually respect fair play. Are your correctives fair, consistent and a logical and realistic response to the behaviour?

THE TOOLS

Check the child's academic ability

Understand exactly where the child is academically and if necessary consider referring her for an assessment, as her motivational problem may be linked to a learning difficulty. This can be done through the school's Special Educational Needs Co-ordinator (SENCO), or equivalent outside the UK.

Positively reinforce

Recognise all efforts and attempts at improving and completing work by praising and positively reinforcing. Pay attention to the child's abilities and not to her shortcomings.

Buddy-up

Where appropriate use a buddy system for completing a set task. Pair up children within the class to support and motivate each other. Friendship groups work particularly well, providing that they stay on task! Compile a buddy list with your class and explain to them that on certain tasks they will be able to work with their chosen buddy. It is important to set clear expectations of behaviour with all the children.

Sand timer

Help focus the child by using a five- or ten-minute sand timer and a tracker sheet. Place the timer in front of her and inform her of the work she needs to complete within the set time. If she completes her work a sticker/stamp is placed on her tracker sheet. When she has received, for example, four stickers/stamps she is rewarded with five minutes' free time.

Reward chart

Reward charts are an effective way to keep children on-task by stamping their themed sheets to get them closer to achieving their target and reward. It is an ideal way to keep a child focused, especially when coupled with a sand timer; for example, her goal is to complete section x of the set task within ten minutes.

Home–school link book

Provide opportunities throughout the day for the child to experience success and send home positive progress notes or set up a home–school link book.

Keep moving

A child who lacks motivation can easily daydream. To avoid this plan for the child to be on- and off-task, so that she is moving around the classroom completing different activities. These activities can be jobs or tasks related to the subject being taught, for example, using the library or laptop to do some research.

Dictionary game

This is a great game to get the children working as a team. The teacher chooses a word from the dictionary and tells the children the first letter of the word, then reads out the definition, for example, the letter 'A', 'a round fruit with firm white flesh and a green, red or yellow skin'. The first table to get the word correct wins, for example, one token each. More tokens can be given for more difficult words and definitions.

Challenging tasks

All lessons must have an element of challenge in order to motivate the children in your class. Setting clear objectives and involving children in the success criteria of what you want them to achieve encourages independence and ownership. Activities which are child led where children are involved in the planning of the lessons will engage and motivate. Children learn in different ways and if we use a variety of learning methods in lessons this will help to sustain interest and to keep children on-task.

Lollipop sticks

Lollipop sticks are a great way to encourage children who don't readily put up their hands to answer questions in class. Write all the children's names on lollipop sticks and divide them into two pots, one pot with the names of children who always put up their hands and the other pot with the names of children who are reluctant to put up their hands. When you want the children to answer questions take a lollipop stick from each pot and say their name. This way you are targeting the children who maybe know the answer but sometimes lack the confidence to put their hand up in class. Everyone's a winner!

Bibliotherapy

To help children understand and learn to manage their feelings introduce them to a range of books, for example, about lacking in motivation. Children sometimes find it easy to relate to characters in a book and this in itself can help them to understand their own problem(s) and develop coping strategies.

The next step

When the behaviour has been identified and a tool has been tried and implemented you may find the behaviour is still being displayed. Here are some suggestions for the next step.

Step 1 Arrange a meeting with the parent(s)/carer(s) to discuss the behaviour and the way forward.

Step 2 Meet with the Special Educational Needs Co-ordinator (SENCO), or equivalent outside the UK, and discuss the possibility of devising an individual behaviour plan with specific measurable targets.

Step 3 Give time for the behaviour to change. Small steps make the biggest changes.

Step 4 Remember that all children are different and one tool does not fit all. Try a variety of different tools to find the best tool for you and your class.

Tool 16

Overcoming Forgetfulness

The behaviour

Children actively process information in their brains as part of their natural development so that it is sometimes difficult for them to recall things which are not important to them.

SELF-ASSESSMENT CHECKLIST

As teachers we are constantly faced with challenges every day and providing solutions to these challenges is not an easy task. Sometimes, however hard we try, certain situations push our professionalism to the limit. When this happens we need to take a deep breath and ask ourselves some basic questions as to why these things are happening.

Here is a simple five-step checklist to do a quick self-assessment for any situation which you may face in the classroom. If you can answer all these questions then you know that you have got the basics covered and can go ahead with finding the right tool to fit the right behaviour. Spending a short time doing this before you implement the tool will ensure that you achieve ultimate success.

Step 1 Check the history

Play detective and find out all you can about the behaviour and the child. It may mean finding out what his behaviour was like the previous year, meeting with his class teacher or phoning up his previous school. Gather as much information as you can. What strategies were previously used? Was there parental involvement? Attendance record? Friendship groups? Academic performance?

Step 2 Check by establishing the 'Why?'

There is always a reason behind every behaviour. Behaviour is a form of communication; sometimes children (and adults) find it difficult to communicate how they are feeling because they don't know what words to use and find it easier to act out the way they feel which can sometimes result in unwanted behaviour. This behaviour is an indication that something is not right and/or their needs are not being met.

By observing and talking to the child and, if appropriate, to his parent(s)/carer(s), you can start to piece together the 'behaviour jigsaw puzzle' in order to create the big picture and establish why he is behaving in this way. When the 'why?' has been established you can then help him to understand and manage that behaviour.

Step 3 Check positive reinforcement

Make sure that the child knows you care about him. Remember that he may have taken a long time to develop this behaviour, so be consistent and patient as the behaviour takes time to change. Establishing a good relationship with a child shows that you are interested in him and promotes his self-esteem. Remember that behaviours occur for a reason and children who display challenging behaviour do not have the skills that adults have in dealing with situations. Are you using positive language? Are your positive reinforcements exciting and motivational? Do your rewards excite and motivate children? Are you consistent in your approach?

Step 4 Check class rules

Rules create clear expectations for children and define what is acceptable behaviour. Are your class rules clear and do all the children in the class understand and respect them? Are they brightly and prominently displayed, and reinforced on a regular basis?

Step 5 Check correctives

Are you consistent in your approach to implementing your correctives within the classroom? Do children see this as fair? Children usually respect fair play. Are your correctives fair, consistent and a logical and realistic response to the behaviour?

THE TOOLS

Memory aids

Help a child design and make laminated visual aids which he can either keep on his desk or in his drawer. These pictorial visual aids can prompt him before a lesson to gather all the equipment he needs, for example, a ruler, pen, pencil and literacy book.

Visual timetable

Create a pictorial laminated visual timetable which will help the child understand the structure of the day, where he needs to be and what equipment he requires. Create a five-day timetable grid and divide up into lessons and break time, then either print off pictures to represent each session or encourage the child to draw them; this way he'll have ownership of it and will be more likely to use the timetable. This provides an excellent prompt to help him remember, prepare ahead and become a more independent learner.

Badges

If a child finds it difficult to remember to do something then get him to design a badge as a reminder, for example, a badge with a picture of money on it to remind him to bring his tuck money for fruit.

Homework policy

At the beginning of the year and/or if a child is frequently not handing in his homework inform his parent(s)/carer(s) of the school's homework policy. If necessary, arrange a meeting and inform them when homework is assigned and when it is handed in. Discuss ways in which school and home can work together to ensure their child completes the task.

Homework buddies

At the start of the school year pair the children up with a homework buddy to ensure all homework is completed and handed in on time. Strategically buddy-up each child who is normally quite forgetful with one who is very responsible and efficient. Introduce scoring cards and every time the buddies hand in their homework on time they score a point. Reward those buddies who have earned the most points over a month.

Two sets

If a child forgets to bring to school equipment, such as a pencil, a rubber and a calculator, arrange a meeting with his parent(s)/carer(s) and ask if he can have two sets: one which he can keep at home and one which he can keep in school.

Bibliotherapy

To help children understand and learn to manage their feelings, introduce them to a range of books, for example, about being forgetful. Children sometimes find it easy to relate to characters in a book and this in itself can help them to understand their own problem(s) and develop coping strategies.

The next step

When the behaviour has been identified and a tool has been tried and implemented you may find the behaviour is still being displayed. Here are some suggestions for the next step.

Step 1 Arrange a meeting with the parent(s)/carer(s) to discuss the behaviour and the way forward.

Step 2 Meet with the Special Educational Needs Co-ordinator (SENCO), or equivalent outside the UK, and discuss the possibility of devising an individual behaviour plan with specific measurable targets.

Step 3 Give time for the behaviour to change. Small steps make the biggest changes.

Step 4 Remember that all children are different and one tool does not fit all. Try a variety of different tools to find the best tool for you and your class.

Tool 17

Addressing Attention-Seeking Behaviour

The behaviour

Providing attention can be a powerful tool in encouraging positive behaviour and reducing unwanted behaviour. Children enjoy receiving attention for a variety of reasons. If certain children do not receive enough positive attention for their good behaviours, they will often resort to behaviour that results in negative forms of attention, for example, making noises, or calling out. Some would prefer to receive this negative attention than to do without attention altogether. Using both positive attention and ignoring the child at the right moments can be very effective. The child soon learns that positive behaviours result in positive attention and negative behaviours result in no attention.

Possible reasons for attention seeking:

- lack of rules and boundaries

- no sense of belonging

- low self-esteem

- a degree of immaturity.

SELF-ASSESSMENT CHECKLIST

As teachers we are constantly faced with challenges every day and providing solutions to these challenges is not an easy task. Sometimes, however hard we try, certain situations push our professionalism to the limit. When this happens we need to take a deep breath and ask ourselves some basic questions as to why these things are happening.

Here is a simple five-step checklist to do a quick self-assessment for any situation which you may face in the classroom. If you can answer all these questions then you know that you have got the basics covered and can go ahead with finding the right tool to fit the right behaviour. Spending a short time doing this before you implement the tool will ensure that you achieve ultimate success.

Step 1 Check the history

Play detective and find out all you can about the behaviour and the child. It may mean finding out what her behaviour was like the previous year, meeting with her class teacher or phoning up her previous school. Gather as much information as you can. What strategies were previously used? Was there parental involvement? Attendance record? Friendship groups? Academic performance?

Step 2 Check by establishing the 'Why?'

There is always a reason behind every behaviour. Behaviour is a form of communication; sometimes children (and adults) find it difficult to communicate how they are feeling because they don't know what words to use and find it easier to act out the way they feel which can sometimes result in unwanted behaviour. This behaviour is an indication that something is not right and/or their needs are not being met.

By observing and talking to the child and, if appropriate, to her parent(s)/carer(s), you can start to piece together the 'behaviour jigsaw puzzle' in order to create the big picture and

establish why she is behaving in this way. When the 'why?' has been established you can then help her to understand and manage that behaviour.

Step 3 Check positive reinforcement

Make sure that the child knows you care about her. Remember that she may have taken a long time to develop this behaviour, so be consistent and patient as the behaviour takes time to change. Establishing a good relationship with a child shows that you are interested in her and promotes her self-esteem. Remember that behaviours occur for a reason and children who display challenging behaviour do not have the skills that adults have in dealing with situations. Are you using positive language? Are your positive reinforcements exciting and motivational? Do your rewards excite and motivate children? Are you consistent in your approach?

Step 4 Check class rules

Rules create clear expectations for children and define what is acceptable behaviour. Are your class rules clear and do all the children in the class understand and respect them? Are they brightly and prominently displayed, and reinforced on a regular basis?

Step 5 Check correctives

Are you consistent in your approach to implementing your correctives within the classroom? Do children see this as fair? Children usually respect fair play. Are your correctives fair, consistent and a logical and realistic response to the behaviour?

THE TOOLS

Top Time

Top Time is a great way to help a child with an attention-seeking behaviour providing it is given consistently on a daily basis. Inform a child at the beginning of the lesson when her Top Time will be and what you expect from her in order for her to have the Top Time. For example, 'Your Top Time will be in half an hour and I expect you to have completed the work which I have set you quietly.' It is important to inform the child how long her Top Time will be and give her plenty of warning before it ends.

Encourage the child to think of activities which she'd like to do with you during Top Time. These activities can be, for example, playing a board game, drawing a picture, icing some biscuits or reading a book. It is important to note that this time is not for you to teach the child but instead to chat, enjoy the interaction of the activity, help if she requests it and to praise her often.

Do not take away Top Time from her but instead, if necessary, take off a minute for every wrong choice she makes leading up to Top Time. This sends a clear message to her that her negative choices, for example, shouting out in class, has led to her losing time taking part in an activity with you.

Positive attention

A child with attention-seeking behaviour will get your attention one way or another. To eliminate the negative attention-seeking behaviour she needs to receive positive attention from you on a regular basis. Motivate her with a few encouraging words. Make eye contact and follow through with a smile or a kind gesture.

Certificates

Certificates can be large or very small and they can be given out at different times of the day to reinforce the positive behaviour which you want to continue to see. They are also very desirable for children as they like to take them home to show to their families, which in itself is another effective reinforcer to continued positive behaviour. During lesson time if you see the child on-task then reward her with a small certificate which reflects how pleased you are with her progress.

Staying on-task

To encourage the child to stay on-task there are a number of things which you can do. Chat with her to establish her understanding of the task, and then praise her for something specific which she is doing, for example, 'You have really captured the texture of that vase in your sketch, well done!' If you are confident that she knows the answer to a question, ask her in front of the class and praise her when she gives the right answer.

Catch her being good

In order to change a behaviour a child needs to know what the desired behaviour is which you'd like to see in class. An effective way to let the child know what is 'good' behaviour is to simply 'catch her being good' before things go wrong, for example, 'Sam, well done, instead of shouting out you've come and asked me in a quiet voice what you need to do next.' Pay lots of attention when she is behaving well and reward her often.

Acceptable behaviour

Let the child know about the behaviour you like, for example, 'Well done for putting up your hand to answer the question.' Make eye contact with her, give a simple smile or nod of the head. Put more energy and attention into good behaviour than into unwanted behaviour. Give attention immediately following the behaviour that you liked. Try to provide positive attention at least once every five minutes.

Unwanted behaviour

If a child has displayed unwanted behaviour, withhold attention for about 30 seconds; for example, after an unwanted behaviour, she should exhibit at least 30 seconds of good behaviour before you provide her with positive attention.

Ignoring the behaviour

Children with attention-seeking behaviour want the attention regardless of whether it is positive or negative, therefore ignoring the behaviour can be a powerful strategy, as they receive no attention at all. A child soon learns that when she displays unwanted behaviour she receives no attention and because of this realisation the unwanted behaviour soon dwindles. This strategy is, however, only effective if it is coupled with giving her positive attention immediately after she has displayed a positive behaviour.

Ignoring an attention-seeking behaviour can have its drawbacks. The child's behaviour can escalate. This is because she is trying to receive the attention she is used to and is testing the new rules that have changed. The behaviour can disrupt the teaching and learning within the classroom. Other children may repeatedly bring the behaviour to your attention.

Not all attention-seeking behaviours can be ignored, especially if the behaviour becomes a risk to the health and safety of others. Decide what type and level of behaviour will demand the implementation of a response from you.

Bibliotherapy

To help children understand and learn to manage their feelings introduce them to a range of books, for example, about feeling sad and lonely. Children sometimes find it easy to relate to characters in a book and this in itself can help them to understand their own problem(s) and develop coping strategies.

The next step

When the behaviour has been identified and a tool has been tried and implemented you may find the behaviour is still being displayed. Here are some suggestions for the next step.

Step 1 Arrange a meeting with the parent(s)/carer(s) to discuss the behaviour and the way forward.

Step 2 Meet with the Special Educational Needs Co-ordinator (SENCO), or equivalent outside the UK, and discuss the possibility of devising an individual behaviour plan with specific measurable targets.

Step 3 Give time for the behaviour to change. Small steps make the biggest changes.

Step 4 Remember that all children are different and one tool does not fit all. Try a variety of different tools to find the best tool for you and your class.

Tool 18

Preventing Children from Calling Out

The behaviour

Calling out in class is a common problem facing teachers today. It can disrupt the teacher's concentration on delivering the lesson and the children's concentration. It can prevent other children from participating and may also encourage other unwanted behaviours. It is therefore important to deal with this behaviour at its first onset because if a child is allowed to call out in class other children may be encouraged to do the same in order to get the required attention. Also, if a child calls out to get attention and he has little/nothing to say he can be ridiculed by the rest of the class which can be very damaging to his self-esteem.

Possible reasons a child may call out:

- there is a lack of rules and boundaries

- to seek the attention of the teacher for a reason – the recurrence of this can create difficulties for the teacher

- to gain recognition from his classmates

- he is not aware of the class rules (put your hand up if you have something to say)

- to feel he has accomplished something good especially if he knew the right answer

- in the case of a child with attention deficit disorder it may be because he has poor impulse control and just says what comes into his head without thinking first. He will need help in developing his skills in self-control.

SELF-ASSESSMENT CHECKLIST

As teachers we are constantly faced with challenges every day and providing solutions to these challenges is not an easy task. Sometimes, however hard we try, certain situations push our professionalism to the limit. When this happens we need to take a deep breath and ask ourselves some basic questions as to why these things are happening.

Here is a simple five-step checklist to do a quick self-assessment for any situation which you may face in the classroom. If you can answer all these questions then you know that you have got the basics covered and can go ahead with finding the right tool to fit the right behaviour. Spending a short time doing this before you implement the tool will ensure that you achieve ultimate success.

Step 1 Check the history

Play detective and find out all you can about the behaviour and the child. It may mean finding out what his behaviour was like the previous year, meeting with his class teacher or phoning up his previous school. Gather as much information as you can. What strategies were previously used? Was there parental involvement? Attendance record? Friendship groups? Academic performance?

Step 2 Check by establishing the 'Why?'

There is always a reason behind every behaviour. Behaviour is a form of communication; sometimes children (and adults) find it difficult to communicate how they are feeling because they don't know what words to use and find it easier to act out the way they feel which can sometimes result in unwanted behaviour. This behaviour is an indication that something is not right and/or their needs are not being met.

By observing and talking to the child and, if appropriate, to his parent(s)/carer(s), you can start to piece together the 'behaviour jigsaw puzzle' in order to create the big picture and establish why he is behaving in this way. When the 'why?' has been established you can then help him to understand and manage that behaviour.

Step 3 Check positive reinforcement

Make sure that the child knows you care about him. Remember that he may have taken a long time to develop this behaviour, so be consistent and patient as the behaviour takes time to change. Establishing a good relationship with a child shows that you are interested in him and promotes his self-esteem. Remember that behaviours occur for a reason and children who display challenging behaviour do not have the skills that adults have in dealing with situations. Are you using positive language? Are your positive reinforcements exciting and motivational? Do your rewards excite and motivate children? Are you consistent in your approach?

Step 4 Check class rules

Rules create clear expectations for children and define what is acceptable behaviour. Are your class rules clear and do all the children in the class understand and respect them? Are they brightly and prominently displayed, and reinforced on a regular basis?

Step 5 Check correctives

Are you consistent in your approach to implementing your correctives within the classroom? Do children see this as fair? Children usually respect fair play. Are your correctives fair, consistent and a logical and realistic response to the behaviour?

THE TOOLS

Asking questions

Question-and-answer time in class can often cause children to call out. To avoid this, phrase your questions, 'If you know what day of the week it is, raise your hand.' By saying 'raise your hand' last, they remember what to do and very rarely call out. It is important to note that children do not have to raise their hands in order to answer a question. Be creative and, instead of asking the children to raise their hands, change it to, for example, fold your arms, touch your ear, stand up.

Positively reinforce

Actively look for good behaviour and praise it, especially among children who sometimes find it difficult and end up calling or shouting out. When you see a child getting your attention in the right way, for example, coming up to your desk and asking in a quiet voice, praise him.

Practise voice levels

Younger children need to be taught about different voice levels so that they are able to control whether they need to whisper or shout. Songs are a great way to do this: select songs or rhymes where the children can shout and whisper the lyrics.

I forget

If a child says that he calls out because he is afraid that he will forget what he wants to say, encourage him to write what he wants to say on paper, then put his hand up. Remember to reward him when he displays the correct behaviour.

Signs and signals

To encourage the child not to shout or call out in class teach him a sign or a signal, for example, a red sign when placed on his desk or held up signals that he needs help. These can be as creative as you want them to be, but for effectiveness keep them simple.

Visual prompts

Some children benefit from having a visual prompt to remind them what they need to do, for example, 'Raise your hand if you want to ask a question.' These prompts can be words and pictures or just pictures. They can be laminated and taped to the child's desk or kept in his drawer.

Ignoring the behaviour

Try ignoring those who shout out and instead call on the one child who remembers to, for example, raise his hand. To help the class make the right choice say, 'I'm waiting for someone to raise their hand before I take the answer.'

Bibliotherapy

To help children understand and learn to manage their feelings introduce them to a range of books, for example, about not listening. Children sometimes find it easy to relate to characters in a book and this in itself can help them to understand their own problem(s) and develop coping strategies.

The next step

When the behaviour has been identified and a tool has been tried and implemented you may find the behaviour is still being displayed. Here are some suggestions for the next step.

Step 1 Arrange a meeting with the parent(s)/carer(s) to discuss the behaviour and the way forward.

Step 2 Meet with the Special Educational Needs Co-ordinator (SENCO), or equivalent in the UK, and discuss the possibility of devising an individual behaviour plan with specific measurable targets.

Step 3 Give time for the behaviour to change. Small steps make the biggest changes.

Step 4 Remember that all children are different and one tool does not fit all. Try a variety of different tools to find the best tool for you and your class.

Tool 19

Stopping Children from Making Unwanted Noises

The behaviour

Making noises in class is a typical example of low-level disruption and a structured approach will help minimise and eliminate the problem. A child may hum, click her tongue, or crack her knuckles, for example. These behaviours are distracting to the teacher and to the rest of the children in the class. These behaviours are totally unacceptable and need to be addressed.

Possible reasons a child may make unwanted noises:

- there is a lack of rules and boundaries

- she is seeking attention

- she is stressed or bored and is looking for a subconscious ways to distract herself from it.

SELF-ASSESSMENT CHECKLIST

As teachers we are constantly faced with challenges every day and providing solutions to these challenges is not an easy task. Sometimes, however hard we try, certain situations push our professionalism to the limit. When this happens we need to take a deep breath and ask ourselves some basic questions as to why these things are happening.

Here is a simple five-step checklist to do a quick self-assessment for any situation which you may face in the classroom. If you can answer all these questions then you know that you have got the basics covered and can go ahead with finding the right tool to fit the right behaviour. Spending a short time doing this before you implement the tool will ensure that you achieve ultimate success.

Step 1 Check the history

Play detective and find out all you can about the behaviour and the child. It may mean finding out what her behaviour was like the previous year, meeting with her class teacher or phoning up her previous school. Gather as much information as you can. What strategies were previously used? Was there parental involvement? Attendance record? Friendship groups? Academic performance?

Step 2 Check by establishing the 'Why?'

There is always a reason behind every behaviour. Behaviour is a form of communication; sometimes children (and adults) find it difficult to communicate how they are feeling because they don't know what words to use and find it easier to act out the way they feel which can sometimes result in unwanted behaviour. This behaviour is an indication that something is not right and/or their needs are not being met.

By observing and talking to the child and, if appropriate, to her parent(s)/carer(s), you can start to piece together the 'behaviour jigsaw puzzle' in order to create the big picture and

establish why she is behaving in this way. When the 'why?' has been established you can then help her to understand and manage that behaviour.

Step 3 Check positive reinforcement

Make sure that the child knows you care about her. Remember that she may have taken a long time to develop this behaviour, so be consistent and patient as the behaviour takes time to change. Establishing a good relationship with a child shows that you are interested in her and promotes her self-esteem. Remember that behaviours occur for a reason and children who display challenging behaviour do not have the skills that adults have in dealing with situations. Are you using positive language? Are your positive reinforcements exciting and motivational? Do your rewards excite and motivate children? Are you consistent in your approach?

Step 4 Check class rules

Rules create clear expectations for children and define what is acceptable behaviour. Are your class rules clear and do all the children in the class understand and respect them? Are they brightly and prominently displayed, and reinforced on a regular basis?

Step 5 Check correctives

Are you consistent in your approach to implementing your correctives within the classroom? Do children see this as fair? Children usually respect fair play. Are your correctives fair, consistent and a logical and realistic response to the behaviour?

THE TOOLS

Reward scheme

Check that the child knows that she is making a noise. Some children make noises without realising that they are doing it. Talk to the child about the noises which she is making and sensitively discuss with her the fact that they are not appropriate in class and are disturbing others' learning and concentration. It would be important to emphasise that together both teacher and child will work on raising her awareness of the behaviour and eradicating it through the use of a reward scheme.

The reward scheme to support this approach could be devised together with the child, but a simple toy safe or similar could be placed on her table, which would ideally be near to the teacher to ensure easy access to praise, reward and reminders without doing so publicly across the classroom. Start the process using five-minute intervals, so that if she did not make a noise within five minutes place a token in her safe. Continue this for the duration of the lesson/day, at the end of which she would count her tokens and if she had received the pre-agreed number she would get the overall reward of free time, for example. Again this reward could be decided with the child in order to give her ownership.

If, however, she makes a noise within the five minutes the time must be decreased to three minutes in order to find an achievable target so that she has confidence in her ability to reach it. The time frame would then be increased as she is succeeding it, ideally in increments of five minutes until she completes a whole lesson/day without making a noise.

Bibliotherapy

To help children understand and learn to manage their feelings introduce them to a range of books, for example, about feeling bored. Children sometimes find it easy to relate to characters in a book and this in itself can help them to understand their own problem(s) and develop coping strategies.

The next step

When the behaviour has been identified and a tool has been tried and implemented you may find the behaviour is still being displayed. Here are some suggestions for the next step.

> Step 1 Arrange a meeting with the parent(s)/carer(s) to discuss the behaviour and the way forward.

Step 2 Meet with the Special Educational Needs Co-ordinator (SENCO), or equivalent outside the UK, and discuss the possibility of devising an individual behaviour plan with specific measurable targets.

Step 3 Give time for the behaviour to change. Small steps make the biggest changes.

Step 4 Remember that all children are different and one tool does not fit all. Try a variety of different tools to find the best tool for you and your class.

PART IV

CONFIDENCE BUILDING

Developing children's confidence is important to help them achieve success; it encourages them to experience new things, trust their own instincts and develop an awareness of their capabilities. Children who lack confidence very often have low self-esteem and find it difficult to forge friendships with their peers inside and outside of school.

A lack of confidence puts children in a more vulnerable position and could cause a child to be led and manipulated easily, resulting in his making inappropriate choices and getting into trouble, for example, bullying, smoking or truancy.

As teachers we need to be aware of this group of children because they are very often the quiet ones in the class who do not draw attention to themselves. The classroom environment will play a big part in supporting this group of children. This needs to be positive so that individual children are not afraid to ask questions or put themselves forward for positions of responsibility such as classroom monitors or a key role in a school play. In order to achieve this classrooms need to build in opportunities for it to happen so that teachers are giving their attention to all the children in the class and not just those displaying challenging behaviour. If we promote this we will have children who make a valid contribution to the classroom and children who feel valued.

Children who are confident:

- are able to problem solve
- take responsibility for their actions
- regulate their emotions and feelings
- can think independently
- take on new challenges
- have a positive outlook.

Tool 20

Supporting the Child Who Lacks Self-Esteem

The behaviour

One of the most important things that as teachers we are constantly trying to promote is getting children to believe in themselves. It's important that children feel accepted and cared for by adults and their peers. Giving children confidence through support and praise raises self-esteem and helps children feel good about themselves. How children perceive themselves affects their motivation, attitude and behaviour.

Children who have low self-esteem feel worthless and feel that the people around them don't care for them or want them to be safe. From when babies are born, they receive the love and care they need by being held and interacting with adults. As they grow they develop the need for a sense of belonging to make them feel part of a community such as their family and school. Creating a 'can do' culture within your classroom will help promote self-esteem.

SELF-ASSESSMENT CHECKLIST

As teachers we are constantly faced with challenges every day and providing solutions to these challenges is not an easy task. Sometimes, however hard we try, certain situations push our professionalism to the limit. When this happens we need to take a deep breath and ask ourselves some basic questions as to why these things are happening.

Here is a simple five-step checklist to do a quick self-assessment for any situation which you may face in the classroom. If you can answer all these questions then you know that you have got the basics covered and can go ahead with finding the right tool to fit the right behaviour. Spending a short time doing this before you implement the tool will ensure that you achieve ultimate success.

Step 1 Check the history

Play detective and find out all you can about the behaviour and the child. It may mean finding out what her behaviour was like the previous year, meeting with her class teacher or phoning up her previous school. Gather as much information as you can. What strategies were previously used? Was there parental involvement? Attendance record? Friendship groups? Academic performance?

Step 2 Check by establishing the 'Why?'

There is always a reason behind every behaviour. Behaviour is a form of communication; sometimes children (and adults) find it difficult to communicate how they are feeling because they don't know what words to use and find it easier to act out the way they feel which can sometimes result in unwanted behaviour. This behaviour is an indication that something is not right and/or their needs are not being met.

By observing and talking to the child and, if appropriate, to her parent(s)/carer(s), you can start to piece together the 'behaviour jigsaw puzzle' in order to create the big picture and

establish why she is behaving in this way. When the 'why?' has been established you can then help her to understand and manage that behaviour.

Step 3 Check positive reinforcement

Make sure that the child knows you care about her. Remember that she may have taken a long time to develop this behaviour, so be consistent and patient as the behaviour takes time to change. Establishing a good relationship with a child shows that you are interested in her and promotes her self-esteem. Remember that behaviours occur for a reason and children who display challenging behaviour do not have the skills that adults have in dealing with situations. Are you using positive language? Are your positive reinforcements exciting and motivational? Do your rewards excite and motivate children? Are you consistent in your approach?

Step 4 Check class rules

Rules create clear expectations for children and define what is acceptable behaviour. Are your class rules clear and do all the children in the class understand and respect them? Are they brightly and prominently displayed, and reinforced on a regular basis?

Step 5 Check correctives

Are you consistent in your approach to implementing your correctives within the classroom? Do children see this as fair? Children usually respect fair play. Are your correctives fair, consistent and a logical and realistic response to the behaviour?

THE TOOLS

Feelings diary

Children who have low self-esteem and lack confidence can sometimes have mood swings. Create a feelings diary and ask the child to record down when she is feeling happy, sad, upset, angry or frustrated. It is important to ask her what happened to make her feel angry, happy, etc., as this will help her to identify the triggers and develop coping strategies. This diary can be used at home and school.

I'm good at...

Find out what the child is good at, for example, football, reading, drawing and give her the opportunity in class to show her skill both to your and to her friends. Encourage her to talk about what she is good at and buddy her up with another child whom she can teach.

Show and tell

Encourage the children to bring in something from home which interests them or illustrates what they have achieved to show the class. This can be done during circle time or at the end of the day. This activity not only makes the child feel important but also builds her confidence.

Look what I can do!

Every week choose a funny activity for the class to do and record everyone's score on a class graph, for example, how long can you balance a ball on your head. This is a great way to find out other things children are good at however bizarre they may be.

Pupil of the week

At the end of the week randomly select a child for 'Pupil of the week'; this makes a great end to the week and gives the opportunity to acknowledge a child's positive contributions in front of the whole class. The child's photo and name is placed on the 'Pupil of the week' board and she receives a certificate and a VIP pass which can allow her to have special privileges the following week, for example, to have afternoon tea with the headteacher.

What do you like about...?

This is a great activity to encourage the children to think about one thing they like about every member of the class (including staff). Get the children to think about the following before deciding what to write:

- What is he good at?
- What did he do to help me?
- How did it make me feel?
- What does he try hard at?

This work can be displayed along with each child's photograph in the classroom, a great way to reinforce how important they all are.

Display it!

Every child is good at something and it's our job as a teacher to identify her talent and in doing so build her self-esteem. On a display board take a photo of each child and underneath her photo write what she is good at, for example, football.

Prefect

For the older child, a great way to boost self-esteem is to make her a prefect with a clear responsibility, for example, helping the younger children during lunchtime in the dinner hall and on the playground. Positively reinforce her efforts on a regular basis.

Bibliotherapy

To help children understand and learn to manage their feelings introduce them to a range of books, for example, about learning to feel good about themselves. Children sometimes find it easy to relate to characters in a book and this in itself can help them to understand their own problem(s) and develop coping strategies.

The next step

When the behaviour has been identified and a tool has been tried and implemented you may find the behaviour is still being displayed. Here are some suggestions for the next step.

Step 1 Arrange a meeting with the parent(s)/carer(s) to discuss the behaviour and the way forward.

Step 2 Meet with the Special Educational Needs Co-ordinator (SENCO), or equivalent outside the UK, and discuss the possibility of devising an individual behaviour plan with specific measurable targets.

Step 3 Give time for the behaviour to change. Small steps make the biggest changes.

Step 4 Remember that all children are different and one tool does not fit all. Try a variety of different tools to find the best tool for you and your class.

Tool 21

Supporting the Child Who Lacks Friends

The behaviour

Friends not only provide companionship but they are also fundamentally important to a child's development. These interactions help with social skills, self-regulation, problem solving and emotional growth. If a child is rejected by his peers this can be very detrimental and can bring about loneliness, low self-esteem, discontentment and a lack of motivation. Therefore forming good friendships with others is invaluable otherwise school can be seen as a very stressful and unappealing place which could lead to absenteeism or other unwanted behaviour.

SELF-ASSESSMENT CHECKLIST

As teachers we are constantly faced with challenges every day and providing solutions to these challenges is not an easy task. Sometimes, however hard we try, certain situations push our professionalism to the limit. When this happens we need to take a deep breath and ask ourselves some basic questions as to why these things are happening.

Here is a simple five-step checklist to do a quick self-assessment for any situation which you may face in the classroom. If you can answer all these questions then you know that you have got the basics covered and can go ahead with finding the right tool to fit the right behaviour. Spending a short time doing this before you implement the tool will ensure that you achieve ultimate success.

Step 1 Check the history

Play detective and find out all you can about the behaviour and the child. It may mean finding out what his behaviour was like the previous year, meeting with his class teacher or phoning up his previous school. Gather as much information as you can. What strategies were previously used? Was there parental involvement? Attendance record? Friendship groups? Academic performance?

Step 2 Check by establishing the 'Why?'

There is always a reason behind every behaviour. Behaviour is a form of communication; sometimes children (and adults) find it difficult to communicate how they are feeling because they don't know what words to use and find it easier to act out the way they feel which can sometimes result in unwanted behaviour. This behaviour is an indication that something is not right and/or their needs are not being met.

By observing and talking to the child and, if appropriate, to his parent(s)/carer(s), you can start to piece together the 'behaviour jigsaw puzzle' in order to create the big picture and establish why he is behaving in this way. When the 'why?' has been established you can then help him to understand and manage that behaviour.

Step 3 Check positive reinforcement

Make sure that the child knows you care about him. Remember that he may have taken a long time to develop this behaviour, so be consistent and patient as the behaviour takes time to change. Establishing a good relationship with a child shows that you are interested in him and promotes his self-esteem. Remember that behaviours occur for a reason and children who display challenging behaviour do not have the skills that adults have in dealing with situations. Are you using positive language? Are your positive reinforcements exciting and motivational? Do your rewards excite and motivate children? Are you consistent in your approach?

Step 4 Check class rules

Rules create clear expectations for children and define what is acceptable behaviour. Are your class rules clear and do all the children in the class understand and respect them? Are they displayed brightly and prominently, and reinforced on a regular basis?

Step 5 Check correctives

Are you consistent in your approach to implementing your correctives within the classroom? Do children see this as fair? Children usually respect fair play. Are your correctives fair, consistent and a logical and realistic response to the behaviour?

THE TOOLS

Friendship groups

Playtimes can be a very lonely time, so identify a few children within the class or throughout the school whom you feel would appeal to the child who is lacking friends. Lasting friendships can be formed when children are interested in the same activities.

Seating arrangements

Sit the child next to someone who has a similar personality and who shares a similar interest. Encourage him to talk and to share his interests at appropriate times during the day. It may also help if he is seated close to you so that the situation can be monitored and reassurance given.

Shared responsibility

Pair the child up with another child in the class to share a job, for example, looking after the class hamster. Encourage the children to work together and where possible positively reinforce when you see values such as co-operation, respect and friendship taking place.

Lunchtime club

A lunchtime or nurture club is a great way for children who find it more difficult to socialise in large open spaces such as the playground to have the opportunity to play and interact in a small group situation. Playing simple board games which encourage interaction and talk build confidence and self-esteem.

After-school clubs

These structured activities are an effective way to connect the child with his peers. Inform the child of all activities taking place after school and buddy him up with another child who is already taking part. This is also an opportunity for children to try something new and to learn a new skill.

Play dates

To strengthen a new friendship suggest 'play dates' to the child's parents/carers when he can invite the new friend home to take part in common interests, for example, playing on the PlayStation or taking part in a craft activity.

Act of kindness book

Introduce an 'Act of kindness book' in your class and place it somewhere where everyone can view it. If a child demonstrates an act of kindness then write it in the book: note the kindness that was shown and how the person felt. Encourage children to write in the book themselves. The book can be used to demonstrate and reward positive behaviour.

Bibliotherapy

To help children understand and learn to manage their feelings introduce them to a range of books, for example, about feeling lonely. Children sometimes find it easy to relate to characters in a book and this in itself can help them to understand their own problem(s) and develop coping strategies.

The next step

When the behaviour has been identified and a tool has been tried and implemented you may find the behaviour is still being displayed. Here are some suggestions for the next step.

Step 1 Arrange a meeting with the parent(s)/carer(s) to discuss the behaviour and the way forward.

Step 2 Meet with the Special Educational Needs Co-ordinator (SENCO), or equivalent outside the UK, and discuss the possibility of devising an individual behaviour plan with specific measurable targets.

Step 3 Give time for the behaviour to change. Small steps make the biggest changes.

Step 4 Remember that all children are different and one tool does not fit all. Try a variety of different tools to find the best tool for you and your class.

Tool 22

Addressing Lying

The behaviour

Children who avoid telling the truth find it difficult to give eye contact and generally show tell-tale signs through their body language, for example, by shuffling their feet, hunching their shoulders or putting their hands in their pockets and looking down. In some instances a child who does not give direct contact could be using this to think about the situation before giving a response. Part of our role is to encourage children to make the right choices when they are faced with difficult situations. It is only by being consistent with this positive approach that children realise that it is better to tell the truth and to make the right choice than to lie. Here are some reasons why children lie:

- fear of what the reaction may be
- habit
- presuming what the outcome may be
- modelling by experiencing the lies of others
- to enhance self-esteem
- to avoid blame and/or punishment.

SELF-ASSESSMENT CHECKLIST

As teachers we are constantly faced with challenges every day and providing solutions to these challenges is not an easy task. Sometimes, however hard we try, certain situations push our professionalism to the limit. When this happens we need to take a deep breath and ask ourselves some basic questions as to why these things are happening.

Here is a simple five-step checklist to do a quick self-assessment for any situation which you may face in the classroom. If you can answer all these questions then you know that you have got the basics covered and can go ahead with finding the right tool to fit the right behaviour. Spending a short time doing this before you implement the tool will ensure that you achieve ultimate success.

Step 1 Check the history

Play detective and find out all you can about the behaviour and the child. It may mean finding out what her behaviour was like the previous year, meeting with her class teacher or phoning up her previous school. Gather as much information as you can. What strategies were previously used? Was there parental involvement? Attendance record? Friendship groups? Academic performance?

Step 2 Check by establishing the 'Why?'

There is always a reason behind every behaviour. Behaviour is a form of communication; sometimes children (and adults) find it difficult to communicate how they are feeling because they don't know what words to use and find it easier to act out the way they feel which can sometimes result in unwanted behaviour. This behaviour is an indication that something is not right and/or their needs are not being met.

By observing and talking to the child and, if appropriate, to her parent(s)/carer(s), you can start to piece together the 'behaviour jigsaw puzzle' in order to create the big picture and

establish why she is behaving in this way. When the 'why?' has been established you can then help her to understand and manage that behaviour.

Step 3 Check positive reinforcement

Make sure that the child knows you care about her. Remember that she may have taken a long time to develop this behaviour, so be consistent and patient as the behaviour takes time to change. Establishing a good relationship with a child shows that you are interested in her and promotes her self-esteem. Remember that behaviours occur for a reason and children who display challenging behaviour do not have the skills that adults have in dealing with situations. Are you using positive language? Are your positive reinforcements exciting and motivational? Do your rewards excite and motivate children? Are you consistent in your approach?

Step 4 Check class rules

Rules create clear expectations for children and define what is acceptable behaviour. Are your class rules clear and do all the children in the class understand and respect them? Are they brightly and prominently displayed, and reinforced on a regular basis?

Step 5 Check correctives

Are you consistent in your approach to implementing your correctives within the classroom? Do children see this as fair? Children usually respect fair play. Are your correctives fair, consistent and a logical and realistic response to the behaviour?

THE TOOLS

Attention-seeking behaviour

If you think the child is lying to gain your attention then providing the situation isn't serious ignore the behaviour. Focus on catching any signs of honesty, however small, that the child displays during the day and acknowledge these and positively reinforce, for example, 'Beth well done for telling Arron the truth about using his pencil sharpener without permission and I admire you for telling him you'll ask him next time before you use it.' This way she will be less likely to lie to gain your attention.

Don't overreact

If a child does not tell you the truth, don't overreact as this can cause her to become very skilful in lying and the behaviour can become deep rooted. Instead, approach the child in a calm and assertive way, create an environment in which she can feel safe and secure as this will encourage her to trust you and open up. It is important that she acknowledges the lie and receives the appropriate level of corrective.

What if...?

Put children in small groups and give them a series of hypothetical situations to discuss; for example, Ayan was playing football with his friends and he kicked the ball and accidentally smashed a window. How do you think he feels? What should he do? Should he tell the truth or lie? What do you think will happen if he tells the truth? What do you think will happen if he lies?

Positive talk

Throughout the year use the phrase, 'Thank you for being honest' when a child tells the truth. This can be reinforced on a one-to-one basis or with the whole class, as peer pressure is a very powerful tool in exerting behaviour change. If a child admits to an incident then praise her honesty and implement an appropriate corrective for the behaviour. Don't call a child a liar as this can reinforce the behaviour and encourage a negative response.

Don't ignore

Do not ignore a child who is lying about an incident as there may be an underlying cause to her lying and if this is the case a meeting with her parent(s)/carer(s) is recommended to help establish the reason. Always be aware that there may be a child protection issue as to why a child is lying! Refer to the school's child protection guidelines if this is the case.

Honesty box

To encourage children to tell the truth, ask them to design an honesty box with slips of paper stored at the side. If/when there's an incident which requires a child to tell the truth encourage her to write her comments and name on one of the slips of paper and post it in the honesty box. You can then read through what each child has written and if the culprit has told the truth this can be addressed at your discretion.

The Boy who cried 'Wolf!'

As a class, read Aesop's classic fable 'The Boy who cried "Wolf!"' about a young shepherd boy who kept villagers running to help him by screaming that a wolf was chasing his flock of sheep. But when a wolf really did scare his flock, none of the villagers came to his rescue and the sheep ran away because no one believed him any more.

- Why do you think the shepherd boy lied?
- How do you think the shepherd boy felt when the villagers didn't help him?
- How do you think the villagers felt when the shepherd boy told the truth and they didn't help him?
- What do you think the shepherd boy did to regain the trust of the villagers?

What does honesty mean?

As a class, discuss what you think being honest means. Should you always tell the truth? Why/why not? Talk about how you would feel if you found out someone hasn't been totally honest with you. Do you think it is important to be honest? Do you expect other people to be honest with you?

Question with care

Avoid asking direct questions, as these can encourage a child to lie, for example, 'Did you swear at Jake?' Instead, ask the child to retell the sequence of events leading up to the incident; this not only gives you more of an understanding about what has happened, but it will also identify the trigger which allegedly caused the behaviour. While she is retelling the sequence of events, observe her verbal and non-verbal expressions. Gather as much evidence as possible by questioning other children and staff to build up a complete picture. If you are not convinced that the child is telling the truth, rather than saying, 'That's a lie', say, 'I hear what you're saying, but are you sure that's what happened?'

Mistakes

Reassure the children that we all make mistakes as they can be viewed as portals to learning. As humans we all make mistakes and these should be seen as a valuable and effective way to learn. When a mistake has been made the child must be encouraged to see it as a valuable learning process and helped to decide how to resolve the issue.

Bibliotherapy

To help children understand and learn to manage their feelings introduce them to a range of books, for example, about telling the truth. Children sometimes find it easy to relate to characters in a book and this in itself can help them to understand their own problem(s) and develop coping strategies.

The next step

When the behaviour has been identified and a tool has been tried and implemented you may find the behaviour is still being displayed. Here are some suggestions for the next step.

Step 1 Arrange a meeting with the parent(s)/carer(s) to discuss the behaviour and the way forward.

Step 2 Meet with the Special Educational Needs Co-ordinator (SENCO), or equivalent in the UK, and discuss the possibility of devising an individual behaviour plan with specific measurable targets.

Step 3 Give time for the behaviour to change. Small steps make the biggest changes.

Step 4 Remember that all children are different and one tool does not fit all. Try a variety of different tools to find the best tool for you and your class.

Tool 23

Supporting the Child Who Is Frequently Crying

The behaviour

Crying is one way that children express their emotions, although seeing a child cry can be quite stressful for those involved. Younger children cry more often as this is their way of communicating their emotions, particularly if they have been hurt. As a child progresses through the school he cries less often and crying will be for a specific thing.

There are many reasons why a child might cry:

- start of a new school
- if he doesn't feel well
- attention-seeking
- frustration
- irritability caused, for example, by lack of sleep
- depression
- bereavement
- bullying
- falling out with his friends
- falling over.

SELF-ASSESSMENT CHECKLIST

As teachers we are constantly faced with challenges every day and providing solutions to these challenges is not an easy task. Sometimes, however hard we try, certain situations push our professionalism to the limit. When this happens we need to take a deep breath and ask ourselves some basic questions as to why these things are happening.

Here is a simple five-step checklist to do a quick self-assessment for any situation which you may face in the classroom. If you can answer all these questions then you know that you have got the basics covered and can go ahead with finding the right tool to fit the right behaviour. Spending a short time doing this before you implement the tool will ensure that you achieve ultimate success.

Step 1 Check the history

Play detective and find out all you can about the behaviour and the child. It may mean finding out what his behaviour was like the previous year, meeting with his class teacher or phoning up his previous school. Gather as much information as you can. What strategies were previously used? Was there parental involvement? Attendance record? Friendship groups? Academic performance?

Step 2 Check by establishing the 'Why?'

There is always a reason behind every behaviour. Behaviour is a form of communication; sometimes children (and adults) find it difficult to communicate how they are feeling because they don't know what words to use and find it easier to act out the way they feel which can sometimes result in unwanted behaviour. This behaviour is an indication that something is not right and/or their needs are not being met.

By observing and talking to the child and, if appropriate, to his parent(s)/carer(s), you can start to piece together the 'behaviour jigsaw puzzle' in order to create the big picture and establish why he is behaving in this way. When the 'why?' has been established you can then help him to understand and manage that behaviour.

Step 3 Check positive reinforcement

Make sure that the child knows you care about him. Remember that he may have taken a long time to develop this behaviour, so be consistent and patient as the behaviour takes time to change. Establishing a good relationship with a child shows that you are interested in him and promotes his self-esteem. Remember that behaviours occur for a reason and children who display challenging behaviour do not have the skills that adults have in dealing with situations. Are you using positive language? Are your positive reinforcements exciting and motivational? Do your rewards excite and motivate children? Are you consistent in your approach?

Step 4 Check class rules

Rules create clear expectations for children and define what is acceptable behaviour. Are your class rules clear and do all the children in the class understand and respect them? Are they brightly and prominently displayed, and reinforced on a regular basis?

Step 5 Check correctives

Are you consistent in your approach to implementing your correctives within the classroom? Do children see this as fair? Children usually respect fair play. Are your correctives fair, consistent and a logical and realistic response to the behaviour?

THE TOOLS

Acknowledge

It is important to acknowledge that the child is upset and has feelings; by doing this he feels listened to and is more likely to tell you why he feels upset. Try not to ask him not to cry as this can have an adverse effect despite your good intentions behind the request.

Meeting with parent(s)/carer(s)

Set up a meeting with the child's family to help gain an understanding of his behaviour. During the meeting encourage the family to 'tell their story' around why they feel their child is behaving in a certain way. This can be an empowering technique for them as they start to identify the reasons behind the crying and in doing so begin to formulate their own strategies. Ask open questions and, if needed, guide and prompt the family by using the following questions:

- Have there been any recent life changes, for example, new baby?
- What are the daily routines, for example, meals, sleep?
- How much quality one-to-one time is spent with your child?
- How do you manage your child's behaviour, for example, rules, correctives, praise?
- Why do you think your child is displaying this type of behaviour?

Once the family have recognised the issues and possible causes, a way forward between home and school can be discussed to help the family provide their child with the correct care, support, skills and direction.

Bibliotherapy

To help children understand and learn to manage their feelings introduce them to a range of books, for example, about feeling upset. Children sometimes find it easy to relate to characters in a book and this in itself can help them to understand their own problem(s) and develop coping strategies.

The next step

When the behaviour has been identified and a tool has been tried and implemented you may find the behaviour is still being displayed. Here are some suggestions for the next step.

Step 1 Arrange a meeting with the parent(s)/carer(s) to discuss the behaviour and the way forward.

Step 2 Meet with the Special Educational Needs Co-ordinator (SENCO), or equivalent outside the UK, and discuss the possibility of devising an individual behaviour plan with specific measurable targets.

Step 3 Give time for the behaviour to change. Small steps make the biggest changes.

Step 4 Remember that all children are different and one tool does not fit all. Try a variety of different tools to find the best tool for you and your class.

PART V

CHALLENGING BEHAVIOUR

If you asked any teacher to prioritise key factors that prevent effective teaching and learning taking place in the classroom, generally they will say challenging behaviour from children. Teachers came into the profession to reach all types of children, but this vision is sometimes difficult to put into practice when teachers are faced with behaviour that impedes the learning and teaching of others. It can cause stress and anxiety for the teacher, particularly when strategies put into place fail to have the desired effect.

Qureshi and Alborz (1992) and Hastings and Remington (1994) defined five types of challenging behaviour. These are:

- aggressive behaviour

- destructive behaviour

- self-injurious behaviour

- stereotype behaviour

- socially or sexually unacceptable behaviours.

So, what do we mean by challenging behaviour? In order to address it we need first of all to be clear about what it means. Emerson *et al.* (1987) were some of the first to define challenging behaviour. Their definition was:

Behaviour of such intensity, frequency and duration that the physical safety of the person or others is likely to be placed in serious jeopardy or behaviour which is likely to seriously limit or delay access to, and use of ordinary facilities.

Unwanted behaviour starts to become a concern if the following increase:

- frequency
- intensity
- duration.

Frequency

The frequency is the rate of re-occurrence at which the unwanted behaviour takes place. If a child, for example, repeatedly disrupts the class she may be seen as exhibiting unacceptable behaviour.

Intensity

The intensity is the level or the seriousness of the unwanted behaviour. For example, Shannon can engage in positive behaviour for weeks. But if she gets angry her behaviour may involve biting, shouting, spitting or hitting another child. The outbursts could cause physical harm as well as upset other children, parents or staff.

Duration

The duration is the length of time for which the unwanted behaviour lasts. For example, Brandon has had a disagreement with a friend. He will not follow his teacher's instructions. He refuses to return to class. When he does he becomes sulky and argumentative. His poor behaviour lasts for over an hour and continually disrupts the class.

All behaviour is relative and situation-specific dependent on individual schools and their settings. Factors that can determine behaviours are the social and economical settings of the school and child, historical factors such as family background and medical reasons. These different contexts determine whether behaviour is appropriate or inappropriate. For example, what is deemed acceptable at home may be unacceptable in the classroom. The purpose of identifying what challenging behaviour is and the reasons behind it are essential in addressing these behaviours. One thing for certain is that these challenging behaviours cannot be allowed to carry on!

Tool 24

Helping the Child Who Is Not Following Direction

The behaviour

It can be very frustrating for teachers if, when giving an instruction, a child refuses to follow a direction or does it when he feels like it and not when he has been asked to do something. This can leave you with a feeling of humiliation and resentment as to why this has happened. It also shows a real lack of respect for authority and a disregard of any class rules or boundaries that have been created. Children who challenge you by not following a direction may do so for the following reasons:

- something has upset them
- they feel that an incident has been dealt with unfairly
- they feel angry
- they feel that class rules are not for them
- they feel insecure
- relationships have broken down.

SELF-ASSESSMENT CHECKLIST

As teachers we are constantly faced with challenges every day and providing solutions to these challenges is not an easy task. Sometimes, however hard we try, certain situations push our professionalism to the limit. When this happens we need to take a deep breath and ask ourselves some basic questions as to why these things are happening.

Here is a simple five-step checklist to do a quick self-assessment for any situation which you may face in the classroom. If you can answer all these questions then you know that you have got the basics covered and can go ahead with finding the right tool to fit the right behaviour. Spending a short time doing this before you implement the tool will ensure that you achieve ultimate success.

Step 1 Check the history

Play detective and find out all you can about the behaviour and the child. It may mean finding out what his behaviour was like the previous year, meeting with his class teacher or phoning up his previous school. Gather as much information as you can. What strategies were previously used? Was there parental involvement? Attendance record? Friendship groups? Academic performance?

Step 2 Check by establishing the 'Why?'

There is always a reason behind every behaviour. Behaviour is a form of communication; sometimes children (and adults) find it difficult to communicate how they are feeling because they don't know what words to use and find it easier to act out the way they feel which can sometimes result in unwanted behaviour. This behaviour is an indication that something is not right and/or their needs are not being met.

By observing and talking to the child and, if appropriate, to his parent(s)/carer(s), you can start to piece together the 'behaviour jigsaw puzzle' in order to create the big picture and establish why he is behaving in this way. When the 'why?' has been established you can then help him to understand and manage that behaviour.

Step 3 Check positive reinforcement

Make sure that the child knows you care about him. Remember that he may have taken a long time to develop this behaviour, so be consistent and patient as the behaviour takes time to change. Establishing a good relationship with a child shows that you are interested in him and promotes his self-esteem. Remember that behaviours occur for a reason and children who display challenging behaviour do not have the skills that adults have in dealing with situations. Are you using positive language? Are your positive reinforcements exciting and motivational? Do your rewards excite and motivate children? Are you consistent in your approach?

Step 4 Check class rules

Rules create clear expectations for children and define what is acceptable behaviour. Are your class rules clear and do all the children in the class understand and respect them? Are they brightly and prominently displayed, and reinforced on a regular basis?

Step 5 Check correctives

Are you consistent in your approach to implementing your correctives within the classroom? Do children see this as fair? Children usually respect fair play. Are your correctives fair, consistent and a logical and realistic response to the behaviour?

THE TOOLS

Scripts

The use of scripts are effective in a number of ways: first, they provide a direct, consistent and fair response to encourage the child to follow your direction; second, they provide him with a familiar procedure in response to his behaviour which ultimately helps him to make the right choice; and third, they prevent you from showing the child a route map to your emotions.

Below are two examples of a script used for a child who is calm and for a child who is not calm:

An example script to respond to a child in a calm state:

> Approach the child, get down to his eye level and say 'I'm asking you for the first time to line up with the class.' Move away from the child immediately after delivering the message giving him plenty of space and wait between 30 to 60 seconds.

> Return to the child, get down to his eye level and say, 'I'm asking you for the second time to line up with the class. Remember if you do not follow my direction when I ask you the third time you will miss five minutes of your playtime.' Move away from the child immediately after delivering the message giving him plenty of space and wait between 30 to 60 seconds.

> Return to the child, get down to his eye level and say, 'I'm asking you for the third time to line up with the class.' If he follows the direction praise him for doing so; if he does not follow the direction, follow through with the corrective.

An example script to respond to a child *not* in a calm state:

> From a distance, say to the child, 'I can see you are angry, I'm going to give you a few minutes to calm down then I'm going to ask you to follow my direction.' Move away from him immediately after delivering the message, giving him plenty of space and wait until he has calmed down. This could take between five to ten minutes or longer. If he is becoming a risk to himself or others, then seek help and advice from a senior member of staff.

> Approach the child when he is calm, get down to his eye level and say, 'I'm asking you for the first time to line up with the class.' Move away from him immediately after delivering the message giving him plenty of space and wait between 30 to 60 seconds.

Return to the child, get down to his eye level and say, 'I'm asking you for the second time to line up with the class. Remember if you do not follow my direction when I ask you the third time you will miss five minutes of your playtime.' Move away from the child immediately after delivering the message giving him plenty of space and wait between 30 to 60 seconds.

Return to the child, get down to his eye level and say, 'I'm asking you for the third time to line up with the class.' If he follows the direction, praise him for doing so, if he does not follow the direction, follow through with the corrective.

Choices

Giving a child a choice if/when he is not following your direction can prove very effective as it is very difficult to argue when someone has given you a choice. For example, if a child is playing with his toy car during lesson time, approach him, get down to his eye level and say, 'Christopher, either put the car in your drawer or put it on my desk, thank you.' Move away from him immediately after delivering the choice giving him plenty of space to think about making the right choice. If the child continues to play with the car follow the scripts above.

Visual signs

For some children the use of visual signs can help them to understand appropriate and inappropriate behaviour. A card system is an effective way to achieve this giving the child a three-step process; for example, when he starts to display unwanted behaviour a yellow card is shown, if he continues with the behaviour an orange card is shown, and if he still persists with the behaviour a red card is shown. When the red card is shown the child receives the corrective realistic to the behaviour displayed.

Bibliotherapy

To help children understand and learn to manage their feelings introduce them to a range of books, for example, about feeling angry. Children sometimes find it easy to relate to characters in a book and this in itself can help them to understand their own problem(s) and develop coping strategies.

The next step

When the behaviour has been identified and a tool has been tried and implemented you may find the behaviour is still being displayed. Here are some suggestions for the next step.

Step 1 Arrange a meeting with the parent(s)/carer(s) to discuss the behaviour and the way forward.

Step 2 Meet with the Special Educational Needs Co-ordinator (SENCO), or equivalent outside the UK, and discuss the possibility of devising an individual behaviour plan with specific measurable targets.

Step 3 Give time for the behaviour to change. Small steps make the biggest changes.

Step 4 Remember that all children are different and one tool does not fit all. Try a variety of different tools to find the best tool for you and your class.

Tool 25

Reforming Aggressive Behaviour

The behaviour

An angry child often lacks the inner self-control to deal with her anger and may also lack the ability to express her feelings verbally. She may display anger by becoming withdrawn and unresponsive towards her peers and teacher, or fly off the handle and lash out verbally or physically.

Possible reasons for aggressive behaviour:

- build-up of frustration

- being bullied

- not being understood

- lack of justice and fairness

- lacking in confidence.

SELF-ASSESSMENT CHECKLIST

As teachers we are constantly faced with challenges every day and providing solutions to these challenges is not an easy task. Sometimes, however hard we try, certain situations push our professionalism to the limit. When this happens we need to take a deep breath and ask ourselves some basic questions as to why these things are happening.

Here is a simple five-step checklist to do a quick self-assessment for any situation which you may face in the classroom. If you can answer all these questions then you know that you have got the basics covered and can go ahead with finding the right tool to fit the right behaviour. Spending a short time doing this before you implement the tool will ensure that you achieve ultimate success.

Step 1 Check the history

Play detective and find out all you can about the behaviour and the child. It may mean finding out what her behaviour was like the previous year, meeting with her class teacher or phoning up her previous school. Gather as much information as you can. What strategies were previously used? Was there parental involvement? Attendance record? Friendship groups? Academic performance?

Step 2 Check by establishing the 'Why?'

There is always a reason behind every behaviour. Behaviour is a form of communication; sometimes children (and adults) find it difficult to communicate how they are feeling because they don't know what words to use and find it easier to act out the way they feel which can sometimes result in unwanted behaviour. This behaviour is an indication that something is not right and/or their needs are not being met.

By observing and talking to the child and, if appropriate, to her parent(s)/carer(s), you can start to piece together the 'behaviour jigsaw puzzle' in order to create the big picture and establish why she is behaving in this way. When the 'why?' has been established you can then help her to understand and manage that behaviour.

Step 3 Check positive reinforcement

Make sure that the child knows you care about her. Remember that she may have taken a long time to develop this behaviour, so be consistent and patient as the behaviour takes time to change. Establishing a good relationship with a child shows that you are interested in her and promotes her self-esteem. Remember that behaviours occur for a reason and children who display challenging behaviour do not have the skills that adults have in dealing with situations. Are you using positive language? Are your positive reinforcements exciting and motivational? Do your rewards excite and motivate children? Are you consistent in your approach?

Step 4 Check class rules

Rules create clear expectations for children and define what is acceptable behaviour. Are your class rules clear and do all the children in the class understand and respect them? Are they brightly and prominently displayed, and reinforced on a regular basis?

Step 5 Check correctives

Are you consistent in your approach to implementing your correctives within the classroom? Do children see this as fair? Children usually respect fair play. Are your correctives fair, consistent and a logical and realistic response to the behaviour?

THE TOOLS

Responding to an incident

Responding correctly to a child displaying aggressive behaviour is vitally important to avoid a situation getting out of control. Always address the behaviour and follow through, to gain the child's respect. But before this can happen you must begin to understand what has caused the behaviour to ensure an effective and positive outcome. Always remember to separate the child from the inappropriate behaviour and try hard never to take a child's behaviour personally. All children are unique and because of this a 'treatment for all' is not the best approach. Instead, children must be responded to according to their individual needs.

Dealing with an incident

When dealing with a situation it is important to wait for a child to calm down fully, to get back to the 'baseline', before discussing the incident. This prevents the situation from escalating out of control. The time–intensity model (Smith 1993) illustrates the course of an anger-fuelled behavioural incident.

The 'recovery phase' following an incident is a risky time to discuss the incident and to start requesting apologies. This is because it is a time when further incidents are highly likely.

Positive handling

Before any member of staff can positively handle a child it is advisable for her to have appropriate training and follow the school's positive handling policy.

Acknowledge

It is important to acknowledge the child's anger, for example, 'It's OK to feel angry; I can see you're upset about what has happened. I'd like to help you express your anger safely so that no one gets hurt.' Avoid using negative talk, for example, 'Don't be so silly', as this can escalate the anger.

Reflective listening

It is important for you to model a calm and assertive disposition as this will help to prevent the child's anger from escalating. Listen to what she has to say so that she feels that she is being listened to and that you care about her. Repeat back to her (in her words) what she is telling you in a calm and soothing tone, for example, 'I hear what you're saying, Umah, that you got upset when Liam pushed past you in the corridor.' This positively encourages her to start to feel as if she is back in control and ultimately reduces the incidents of an angry outburst. Remain in control.

Identify the signs of anger

Helping a child identify signs of anger is a very useful skill. She becomes more aware regarding how she feels in different situations and becomes more confident in her ability to deal with any feelings of anger. Explore the signs of anger with her, for example, clenched fists, change in facial expressions and voice pitch and tone. When/if a child feels as if she is beginning to get angry encourage her to use coping strategies to help her deal with the situation in a positive and controlled way.

Firework analogy

Talk to the child about anger using a firework analogy with which she can easily identify (Faupel, Herrick and Sharp 1998). Explain to her that what causes her anger is like the match that lights the firework, the way we feel about the trigger is the fuse and the explosion is how we react internally and/or externally. Get her to make or draw a firework and attach to the fuse in words the triggers that can cause her anger, for example, name-calling.

Coping strategies

Coping strategies can help a child to refocus her energy especially when she is angry. These strategies are only effective when they become habitual. Here are some effective coping strategies for anger. Type them onto a card with a symbol next to each one, laminate it and give it to the child so that she can keep it in her pocket and use whenever necessary.

- Walk away from the situation and sit quietly and comfortably.
- Close your eyes and think about your breathing.
- Count your breaths as you are breathing and this will help you to calm down.
- Go and tell a teacher what has made you angry so that they can deal with the situation.

Count to ten

Counting to ten helps reduce anger as it helps to focus the child's breathing and it helps to distract her from the situation that has caused her to feel angry. Help the child count to ten and to take slow deep breaths between each number. This helps to counteract the fight or flight stress reaction that underlies anger. Deliberately taking a slow, deep breath not only brings a soothing sense of relaxation, but will also helps to focus her attention in the present moment.

Empathy

It is important to teach children people-skills such as empathy to help them understand and be sensitive to how other people think and feel (Faupel *et al.* 1998). Using empathy equips the child with the necessary skills to help her to manage her behaviour when faced with potential triggers, for example, if she fails to score a goal on the football pitch. Through personal and social education (PSE) or emotional literacy teach the child empathy. This can be achieved through a number of activities. Choose the appropriate activities to help her to understand other people's feelings and as a result become less aggressive towards them. There are some great activities in Social and Emotional Aspects of Learning (SEAL) (see the list of Resources at the back of the book for details).

Quiet time card

Provide the child with a 'quiet time' card, which she can show when she feels angry. This card allows them 5–10 minutes of quiet time either within the classroom or within a partner classroom. When she shows the card she is rewarded for making the right choice.

Squeeze me!

Give the child a small ball to keep on her desk which she can squeeze every time she feels stressed or angry. This will help to release her anger. Praise and acknowledge her when she makes the right choice and squeezes the ball.

Can you cool off?

Ask the children to find a space and stand with their eyes closed. Ask them to think of something in the past that has made them angry. Ask them to imagine that anger turning into a hot red lump in the centre of their bodies and if they don't do something they will explode. Now ask them to feel soft cold snow falling on their heads. As the snow touches them their bodies absorb it and it begins to cool their anger, and after a while their anger is so cold that it disappears and they are back to normal. Ask the children to use this method next time they feel angry.

Buddy-up

If a child is likely to experience an angry outburst buddy her up with a sensible child from the same class to whom she can talk when she starts to feel angry. Encourage the buddy child to ask her questions to establish the route concern of the anger, for example, 'What happened?', 'Who was involved?', 'What did they do?', 'What did you do?', 'How did you feel?'

Positive reinforcement

When you see a child implementing the skills and tools given to help manage her anger provide immediate positive reinforcement through praise, recognition and/or rewards. This helps to reinforce the positive behaviour and she will be more likely to continue making the right choices.

Bibliotherapy

To help children understand and learn to manage their feelings introduce them to a range of books, for example, about feeling angry. Children sometimes find it easy to relate to characters in a book and this in itself can help them to understand their own problem(s) and develop coping strategies.

The next step

When the behaviour has been identified and a tool has been tried and implemented you may find the behaviour is still being displayed. Here are some suggestions for the next step.

Step 1 Arrange a meeting with the parent(s)/carer(s) to discuss the behaviour and the way forward.

Step 2 Meet with the Special Educational Needs Co-ordinator (SENCO), or equivalent outside the UK, and discuss the possibility of devising an individual behaviour plan with specific measurable targets.

Step 3 Give time for the behaviour to change. Small steps make the biggest changes.

Step 4 Remember that all children are different and one tool does not fit all. Try a variety of different tools to find the best tool for you and your class.

Tool 26

Stopping a Child from Spitting

The behaviour

Spitting is a behaviour which can be done by a child for the following reasons:

- a medical/physical problem
- to look tough
- to express his anger when he doesn't have the vocabulary
- resentment
- anger
- frustration
- frightened of something or someone.

SELF-ASSESSMENT CHECKLIST

As teachers we are constantly faced with challenges every day and providing solutions to these challenges is not an easy task. Sometimes, however hard we try, certain situations push our professionalism to the limit. When this happens we need to take a deep breath and ask ourselves some basic questions as to why these things are happening.

Here is a simple five-step checklist to do a quick self-assessment for any situation which may face in the classroom. If you can answer all these questions then you know that you have got the basics covered and can go ahead with finding the right tool to fit the right behaviour. Spending a short time doing this before you implement the tool will ensure that you achieve ultimate success.

Step 1 Check the history

Play detective and find out all you can about the behaviour and the child. It may mean finding out what his behaviour was like the previous year, meeting with his class teacher or phoning up his previous school. Gather as much information as you can. What strategies were previously used? Was there parental involvement? Attendance record? Friendship groups? Academic performance?

Step 2 Check by establishing the 'Why?'

There is always a reason behind every behaviour. Behaviour is a form of communication; sometimes children (and adults) find it difficult to communicate how they are feeling because they don't know what words to use and find it easier to act out the way they feel which can sometimes result in unwanted behaviour. This behaviour is an indication that something is not right and/or their needs are not being met.

By observing and talking to the child and, if appropriate, to his parent(s)/carer(s), you can start to piece together the 'behaviour jigsaw puzzle' in order to create the big picture and establish why he is behaving in this way. When the 'why?' has been established you can then help him to understand and manage that behaviour.

Step 3 Check positive reinforcement

Make sure that the child knows you care about him. Remember that he may have taken a long time to develop this behaviour, so be consistent and patient as the behaviour takes time to change. Establishing a good relationship with a child shows that you are interested in him and promotes his self-esteem. Remember that behaviours occur for a reason and children who display challenging behaviour do not have the skills that adults have in dealing with situations. Are you using positive language? Are your positive reinforcements exciting and motivational? Do your rewards excite and motivate children? Are you consistent in your approach?

Step 4 Check class rules

Rules create clear expectations for children and define what is acceptable behaviour. Are your class rules clear and do all the children in the class understand and respect them? Are they brightly and prominently displayed, and reinforced on a regular basis?

Step 5 Check correctives

Are you consistent in your approach to implementing your correctives within the classroom? Do children see this as fair? Children usually respect fair play. Are your correctives fair, consistent and a logical and realistic response to the behaviour?

THE TOOLS

Medical concern

If a child is frequently spitting it is advisable to contact his parent(s)/carer(s) in case there is a medical reason, for example, a bronchial problem.

Clean it up!

Our saliva is home to hundreds of harmless bacteria, but if we have an infection it will contain many which *are* harmful. If a child with a cold spits on the playground and another child comes into contact with it and does not wash his hands then this infection can be passed on. If a child deliberately spits on school property it is therefore acceptable to ask him to clean it up; if he refuses then implement the appropriate corrective for the level of behaviour displayed.

Provide alternatives

If a child spits because he feels angry, frustrated or frightened provide him with other ways to express his feelings, for example squeezing a small foam ball. If a child frequently spits as a form of expression, talk about how the act can make people feel and how infections can be passed on. A meeting with his parent(s) or carer(s) would also be advisable.

My mouth

To help reinforce the positive ways we can use our mouths put the children in pairs or groups and ask them to complete each sentence:

'I use my mouth for…'

'I don't use my mouth for spitting because it…'

'I use my mouth for…'

'I don't use my mouth for spitting because it…'

'I use my mouth for…'

'I don't use my mouth for spitting because it…'

Ask each group to read out what they have written; there will be similarities which is great and again can be used to reinforce the key message.

Bibliotherapy

To help children understand and learn to manage their feelings introduce them to a range of books, for example, about feeling frustrated. Children sometimes find it easy to relate to characters in a book and this in itself can help them to understand their own problem(s) and develop coping strategies.

The next step

When the behaviour has been identified and a tool has been tried and implemented you may find the behaviour is still being displayed. Here are some suggestions for the next step.

Step 1 Arrange a meeting with the parent(s)/carer(s) to discuss the behaviour and the way forward.

Step 2 Meet with the Special Educational Needs Co-ordinator (SENCO), or equivalent outside the UK, and discuss the possibility of devising an individual behaviour plan with specific measurable targets.

Step 3 Give time for the behaviour to change. Small steps make the biggest changes.

Step 4 Remember that all children are different and one tool does not fit all. Try a variety of different tools to find the best tool for you and your class.

Tool 27

Addressing Swearing

The behaviour

Swearing in any shape or form is not acceptable in the classroom. Children model their behaviour on adults and if swearing is accepted this does not send the correct message to the children in our class. Some children use swear words as part of their everyday vocabulary outside of school and need to understand that, if this is the case, swearing is not an accepted form of communication within school.

Possible reasons for swearing:

- lack of rules and boundaries
- lack of understanding
- to gain attention
- to make or impress their friends
- to express anger, frustration or fear
- as part of role play, mimicking behaviour in the media
- because they're upset
- to explore cause and effect.

SELF-ASSESSMENT CHECKLIST

As teachers we are constantly faced with challenges every day and providing solutions to these challenges is not an easy task. Sometimes, however hard we try, certain situations push our professionalism to the limit. When this happens we need to take a deep breath and ask ourselves some basic questions as to why these things are happening.

Here is a simple five-step checklist to do a quick self-assessment for any situation which you may face in the classroom. If you can answer all these questions then you know that you have got the basics covered and can go ahead with finding the right tool to fit the right behaviour. Spending a short time doing this before you implement the tool will ensure that you achieve ultimate success.

Step 1 Check the history

Play detective and find out all you can about the behaviour and the child. It may mean finding out what her behaviour was like the previous year, meeting with her class teacher or phoning up her previous school. Find out as much information as you can. What strategies were previously used? Was there parental involvement? Attendance record? Friendship groups? Academic performance?

Step 2 Check by establishing the 'Why?'

There is always a reason behind every behaviour. Behaviour is a form of communication; sometimes children (and adults) find it difficult to communicate how they are feeling because they don't know what words to use and find it easier to act out the way they feel which can sometimes result in unwanted behaviour. This behaviour is an indication that something is not right and/or their needs are not being met.

By observing and talking to the child and, if appropriate, to her parent(s)/carer(s), you can start to piece together the 'behaviour jigsaw puzzle' in order to create the big picture and

establish why she is behaving in this way. When the 'why?' has been established you can then help her to understand and manage that behaviour.

Step 3 Check positive reinforcement

Make sure that the child knows you care about her. Remember that she may have taken a long time to develop this behaviour, so be consistent and patient as the behaviour takes time to change. Establishing a good relationship with a child shows that you are interested in her and promotes her self-esteem. Remember that behaviours occur for a reason and children who display challenging behaviour do not have the skills that adults have in dealing with situations. Are you using positive language? Are your positive reinforcements exciting and motivational? Do your rewards excite and motivate children? Are you consistent in your approach?

Step 4 Check class rules

Rules create clear expectations for children and define what is acceptable behaviour. Are your class rules clear and do all the children in the class understand and respect them? Are they brightly and prominently displayed, and reinforced on a regular basis?

Step 5 Check correctives

Are you consistent in your approach to implementing your correctives within the classroom? Do children see this as fair? Children usually respect fair play. Are your correctives fair, consistent and a logical and realistic response to the behaviour?

THE TOOLS

Reassure

Let the child know it's OK to feel angry, frustrated or frightened, but that swearing is not OK.

Check the child's understanding

Check the child's understanding of the word and why she uses it, ask her what it means. She may think that the word is OK because she has heard her parent(s), carer(s) or friend(s) use it. Help her to understand that these words can hurt other people's feelings.

Provide alternatives

If a child swears because she feels angry, frustrated or frightened, provide her with other ways to express her feelings, for example, ripping a sheet of paper. If a child swears as part of her everyday language, talk about how inappropriate words make people feel and what words can be used instead. A meeting with her parent(s) or carer(s) would also be advisable.

Attention-seeking behaviour

If a child swears for attention inform her in a calm, brief manner that her language is unacceptable and that there are more appropriate ways to gain your attention. See Tool 17 on ' Addressing attention -seeking behaviour'.

Bibliotherapy

To help children understand and learn to manage their feelings introduce them to a range of books, for example, about feeling upset. Children sometimes find it easy to relate to characters in a book and this in itself can help them to understand their own problem(s) and develop coping strategies.

The next step

When the behaviour has been identified and a tool has been tried and implemented you may find the behaviour is still being displayed. Here are some suggestions for the next step.

Step 1 Arrange a meeting with the parent(s)/carer(s) to discuss the behaviour and the way forward.

Step 2 Meet with the Special Educational Needs Co-ordinator (SENCO), or equivalent outside the UK, and discuss the possibility of devising an individual behaviour plan with specific measurable targets.

Step 3 Give time for the behaviour to change. Small steps make the biggest changes.

Step 4 Remember that all children are different and one tool does not fit all. Try a variety of different tools to find the best tool for you and your class.

Resources

Anger management

The Penguin Who Lost her Cool
A story about controlling your anger, by Marla Sobel. New York: Childswork/
Childsplay, 2001

The Koala Who Wouldn't Co-operate
by Lawrence Shapiro. New York: Childswork/Childsplay Early Prevention
Series, 2006

Everybody Gets Angry
by Ellen Pill. Pennsylvania, PA: Bureau for At-risk Youth, 2005

Anger Solution Workbook
by Lisa M. Schab. New York: Childswork/Childsplay, 2001

A Volcano in My Tummy
by Eliane Whitehouse and Warwick Pudney. Canada: New Society Publishers,
1998

Bullying

Anti-Bullying Week
www.antibullyingweek.org

Bully Buster Bingo
by Heidi McDonald. Pennsylvania, PA: Marco Products Inc, 2004

Coping strategies

Coping Strategies for Kids
www.copingskills4kids.net

Emotional literacy

SEAL (Social and Emotional Aspects of Learning)
http://nationalstrategies.standards.dcsf.gov.uk/primary/publications/banda/
seal

Practical Ideas for Emotional Intelligence
by Adele Clark and Jacqui Blades. Milton Keynes: Speechmark Publishing Ltd, 2007

QED Manners
by Kate Tym
Four titles: *Time to Share, Be Nice, Say Please, Tell the Truth*
London: QED Publishing, 2008

Nurturing Game
Creative Productivity Ltd

The Socially Speaking Game
by Alison Schroeder. Nottingham: LDA, 1998

Social Skills (Six board games)
Smartkids (UK) Ltd

Thumball Interactive Game
www.thumball.com

Activities for Group Work with School-age Children
by Susan Ciardiello. Pennsylvania, PA: Marco Products Inc, 2003

Emotions colorcards
Milton Keynes: Speechmark Publishing Ltd, 2008

Feelings

Feelings Series
Oxford: Raintree Publishers

Owning Up (Growing Up)
by Janine Amos. London: Cherry Tree Books

The Huge Bag of Worries
by Virginia Ironside. London: Hodder Children's Books, 2004

Motivation

Free Motivating Daily Quotes
www.MotivatingMates.com

Forgetful Little Fireman
by Alan MacDonald. London: Ladybird Books Ltd, 2007

Positive contact

Massage in Schools
www.massageinschools.com

Team-Teach
www.team-teach.co.uk

Self-esteem

Self-Esteem Games: 300 Fun Activities that Make Children Feel Good about Themselves
by Barbara Sher. Hoboken, NJ: Jossey Bass, 1998

Self-Esteem: Skills to Build Self-Worth
by Amelia Ruscoe. Ireland: Prim Ed, 2006

Self-Esteem: Ideas to Go, Photocopiable Activities
by Tanya Dalgleish. London: A and C Black Publishers Ltd., 2002

Self-Esteem for Boys
by Elizabeth Hartley-Brewer. London: Random House, 2000

Self-Esteem for Girls
by Elizabeth Hartley-Brewer. London: Random House, 2000

Relaxation

Just a Minute CDs
www.just-a-minute.org

Relax for Kids CDs
www.relaxkids.com

Tangles
www.tanglecreations.com

Resources for school

BBC for Schools
Provides learning resources for kids at home and at school.
www.bbc.co.uk/schools

Behaviour 4 Learning
Provides access to research and resources for behaviour management.
www.behaviour4learning.ac.uk

Behaviour Stop Ltd
This (author's website) is first Stop for all your positive behaviour management needs. They provide a hands-on personal approach to creating practical solutions to promote positive relationships for families, schools, adults and children. For 'Kit Bags' full of resources discussed in this book, whole school programmes and courses visit
www.behaviourstop.co.uk

Good Choice Teddy
www.goodchoiceteddy.co.uk

Times Education Supplement
Provides behaviour management strategies in their weekly magazine.
www.tes.co.uk

Values

Family Values Scheme
Effective way to engage parent(s)/carer(s) in their child's personal, social and emotional education.
www.behaviourstop.co.uk/family-values.php

Living Values
Helps students explore and develop positive values and move toward their potential.
www.livingvalues.net

Values Education
A values-based school seeks to promote an educational philosophy based on valuing self, others and the environment through the consideration of an ethical values vocabulary (principles that guide behaviour), as the basis of good educational practice. It encourages adults to model values and to give time for reflective practices that empower individuals to be effective learners and good citizens.
www.values-education.com

Bibliography

Day, C., Sammons, P., Hopkins, D., Leithwood, K. and Kington, A. (2008) 'Research into the impact of school leadership on pupil outcomes: policy and research contexts.' *School Leadership and Management: Special Issue: The Impact of School Leadership on Student Outcomes* 28, 1, 5–25.

Faupel, A., Herrick, E. and Sharp, P. (1998) *Anger Management: A Practical Guide.* London: David Fulton.

Emerson, E., Barnett, S., Bell, C., Cummins, R., McCool, C., Toogood, A. and Mansell, J. (1987) 'Developing services for people with severe learning difficulties and challenging behaviour'. Report of the early work of the Special Development Team in Kent.

Faupel, A. *Emotional Literacy Assessment and Intervention Ages 7–11 Southampton Psychology Service.* London: NFER.

Fay, J. and Funk, D. (1995) *Teaching with Love and Logic.* Golden, CO: The Love and Logic Press Inc.

Geddes, H. (2006) *Attachment in the Classroom.* New York: Worth Publishing.

Gerhardt, S. (2004) *Why Love Matters.* Oxford: Routledge.

Glasser, W. (1986) *Choice Theory in the Classroom.* New York: Harper.

Greene, R.W. (2005) *The Explosive Child.* New York: Harper.

Hastings, R.P. and Remington, B. (1994) 'Rules of engagement: towards an analysis of staff responses to challenging behaviour.' *Research in Developmental Disabilities* 15, 279–298.

Morgan, N.S. (2009) *Quick, Easy and Effective Behaviour Management Ideas for the Classroom.* London: Jessica Kingsley Publishers.

Mortiner, H. (2006) *An A–Z of Tricky Behaviours in the Early Years.* London: QEd Publications.

Qureshi, H. and Alborz, A. (1992) 'The epidemiology of challenging behaviour.' *Mental Handicap Research* 5, 130–145.

Reid, K. (2006) *National Behaviour and Attendance Review (NBAR) Report.* Cardiff: Welsh Assembly Government.

Rosenberg, M.B. (2003) *Nonviolent Communication A Language of Life.* Encinitas, CA: Puddle Dancer Press.

Rosenthal, R. and Jacobson, L. (1992) *Pygmalion in the Classroom.* Carmarthen: Crown House Publishing.

Smith, P. (1993) *Professional Assault Response Training* (2000) (Revised). San Clemente, CA: Professional Growth Facilitators.

Index